# Far From Random

*Using Investor Behavior and Trend Analysis
to Forecast Market Movement*

**RICHARD LEHMAN**

Foreword by Lawrence G. McMillan

BLOOMBERG PRESS
NEW YORK

First edition published 2009

1 3 5 7 9 10 8 6 4 2

Library of Congress Cataloging-in-Publication Data

Lehman, Richard
Far from random: using investor behavior and trend analysis to forecast market movement / Richard Lehman; foreword by Lawrence G. McMillan.
   p. cm.
  Includes bibliographical references and index.
  Summary: "In Far From Random, Lehman uses behavior-based trend analysis to debunk Malkiel's random walk theory. He demonstrates that the market has discernible trends that are foreseeable using trend channel analysis, a form of technical analysis. By learning to spot these trends, investors and traders can predict market movement to boost returns in anything from equities to 401(k) accounts"—Provided by publisher.
  ISBN 978-1-57660-323-9 (alk. paper)
  1. Technical analysis (Investment analysis) 2. Investment analysis. I. Title.
  HG4529.L447 2009
  332.63'2042—dc22

                                                   2009037202

*To Roz and Ed Lehman*
*For 60 years of unwavering support for all my endeavors*

# Contents

**PART III    Charting a Golden Path**

Also by RICHARD LEHMAN

*New Insights on Covered Call Writing:*
*The Powerful Technique That Enhances Return and Lowers Risk in Stock Investing*

Also by BLOOMBERG PRESS

*Market Indicators*
by Richard Sipley

*Breakthroughs in Technical Analysis*
edited by David Keller

*New Thinking in Technical Analysis*
edited by Rick Bensignor

*Technical Analysis Tools*
by Mark Tinghino

*Trading ETFs*
By Deron Wagner

*Trading Option Greeks*
by Dan Passarelli

BLOOMBERG MARKET ESSENTIALS: TECHNICAL ANALYSIS

*DeMark Indicators*
by Jason Perl

*Fibonacci Analysis*
by Constance Brown

*Chart Patterns*
by Bruce M. Kamich

A complete list of our titles is available at
**www/bloomberg.com/books**

# Far From Random

and this book forms a powerful thesis on how to harness this knowledge in a mostly predictive and financially-productive way.

This is an exceptional book for those who are not satisfied with the traditional approach to investing and are seeking ways to enhance their return."

—STEVEN J. FREIBERG
Former co-chairman and CEO of Citigroup's Global Consumer Group

"Can the equity market still be considered efficient after getting sliced in half twice in the same decade? Is this simply a random occurrence? *Far From Random* could not be timelier for what is truly a changed financial market environment, in good part dominated by HFT, mega-flows of levered institutional money, etc. The true marriage of technical and fundamental analysis set against the backdrop of far from perfect or efficient human decision-making isn't a consideration for investors, it's a necessity. Rick has hit the nail on the head. It's time investors finally wake up to a new reality."

—BRIAN PRETTI, CFA, CFP
Chief Investment Officer, Mechanics bank

"In *Far From Random*, we learn we aren't so removed from our ancestors as we might think. This book demonstrates that markets are neither efficient nor random, and that being stone-cold frozen with fear (a saber-tooth tiger eyes us for lunch) is akin to buy-and-hold-no-matter-what (our securities portfolio drags us down to our doom). Richard Lehman boldly states that human emotion, and not green-eyeshade analysis, is what really drives prices. Far from being nonsense, this view makes perfect sense. This book shows how our collective emotional behavior, and the markets it moves, becomes predictable. That's an edge any investor would want, and *Far From Random* will give you a tantalizing glimpse at that edge."

—JIM GLIDDEN
Veteran Wall Street bond salesman

# Foreword

I HAVE ALWAYS believed that technical analysis is by far the most accurate approach for stock market investment. True, my degrees are scientific (math, computer science), so that may have influenced me. But I have conducted many studies of both fundamental and technical approaches in my nearly forty years of investing, and it is the rigorous, technical approach that is the clear winner.

For example, if one buys a stock and it begins to decline, what is one to do? A technician will likely see that the stock is in a down trend (or no longer in an up trend) and will sell the stock, stepping aside until the stock once again is in a rising mode. The fundamental trader, though, supposedly bought the stock because it was cheap, based on some earnings or other fundamental projection. Thus, when it declines in price, he should like it even better, unless something has changed regarding the fundamentals (unlikely). This fundamental approach is in clear conflict with the accepted principle of "cutting one's losses, and letting one's profits run." In fact, as *Far From Random* points out, such an attitude can lead the fundamentalist to feel that he or she is right and the market is wrong—a disastrous attitude for any trader or investor to have.

Most fundamentalists are, in fact, partly technical. In other words, they don't just look at "earnings" but are concerned with things such as the *trend* of earnings or the *price/earnings ratio*. Once "price" or "trend" is introduced into the analysis, one has become a de facto technician.

Exploring the role of technical analysis, *Far From Random* provides a logical and well-constructed approach to the market in general and to stocks in particular. First, the myth that a stock is "worth" something based on its fundamentals is debunked. There is no promise by the corporation to pay anything back to the stockholder as there is to the bondholder. In fact, a stock's worth is much more likely to be the collective opinion of thousands or millions of investors. Those opinions are often subject to emotion—from acmes of greed to nadirs of fear. A stock's price will vary greatly based on those emotions.

The conclusion is that traditional fundamental analysis fails miserably at determining the "fair value" of a stock if there even is such a thing. As a result, most conventional Wall Street advice is useless. This fact was never clearer than in the market decline of 2008. A virtual parade of fundamental analysts kept assuring the public that "stocks were cheap" even as stocks plummeted. The problem was that the marchers in this parade had no real way of knowing what "cheap" was. Technicians, on the other hand, were either out of the market (in cash) or were short because that's the way the price trend was pointing.

*Far From Random* debunks the myth of the efficient market hypothesis (the so-called random walk). Simply stated, that hypothesis is based on the notion that stock prices are governed by rational, knowledgeable (unemotional) people. We know that isn't true, at least at market extremes. Stocks fluctuate in ways that traditional finance cannot predict or explain. Human emotions—fear and greed—play huge roles in the pricing of stocks, and those emotions are nowhere to be seen in either fundamental analysis or the efficient market hypothesis.

The case for technical analysis is made rationally and eloquently in this book. The preferred method of technical analysis is one called *trend channel analysis*. Its objective is to identify the trend and to "ride" it as long as it remains in effect. The logic and attractiveness of such a method should be obvious to all: one stays with winning stocks and exits those that are no longer performing well, with *price* as the arbiter, not earnings.

In fact, it is often said (by technical analysts anyway), that *price* is the ultimate technical or fundamental indicator. If you are following a method that has you fighting the price trend, then it is uncomfortable, emotionally and physically draining, and costs you money. So don't do that. Follow the trend instead.

If you read the pages ahead with an open mind, you will surely see the inadequacies of the traditional Wall Street approach and the benefits of the technical approach. At the very minimum, you should gain an insight to a more logical way of investing with far smaller drawdowns than the traditional "buy and hold" approach—an approach that has been fostered in the United States over the years by brokerage firms and mutual funds, often to the detriment of their own customers.

*Lawrence G. McMillan is President of McMillan Analysis Corp, a derivatives research and money-management firm, and author of the book* Options as a Strategic Investment, *among others.*

# Acknowledgments

I'D LOVE TO have been able to acknowledge the help I received from dozens of people on the completion of this work, but in truth there were only seven. So it is with particular gratitude that I acknowledge the assistance of the following:

Research assistants: Jeremy Chew, BS, UC Berkeley; Laura Graziano, BS, Indiana University, MBA, Santa Clara University; and David Carroll, BA, UC Berkeley

Statistical analysis: James Wang, Economics and Statistics major, UC Berkeley

Special research: Kristen Lehman, BA, University of Texas

Finance advisor: Wayne Price, Finance Instructor, UC Berkeley Extension

Editing: Melissa Honig, BA, UC Irvine, MA, Cal State Northridge, who knows as much about finance as I do about communicative disorders but who proved to be one heck of an editor and a great sport about my obsession with writing this book.

Special thanks to Lawrence McMillan for his Foreword and for the inspiration I have received from his work over many years in both options and technical analysis. Special thanks also to Chip Anderson, President of StockCharts.com, and his staff for the great work they do on their Website.

WITH FEW EXCEPTIONS, authors of financial nonfiction are predominantly PhDs and professors of finance writing on their research or industry practitioners writing about their success. That would make me one of those few exceptions, but then my somewhat unorthodox background is precisely what renders me one of the few people who could see the stock market in the way it is presented in this book.

Since I am not a full-time professor (I teach at night at the University of California at Berkeley Extension), I am neither part of the doctoral mainstream nor affiliated with Berkeley's prestigious Haas School of Business. Therein lies one of my relevant advantages for tackling this subject in that I am not compelled to tow the party line on academia's view of the financial world or what is acceptable to publish. When I was looking for research associates for the book, I spoke with a recent graduate of the Haas School's Masters in Financial Engineering (MFE) program, a unique new curriculum designed to satiate Wall Street's growing appetite for superquantitative analysts. He was interested in working with me until he found out the main subjects included behavioral finance and technical analysis. He said they don't teach either subject in the MFE program and that the thrust of my book would conflict with the financial principles he was taught in school.

MBAs on Wall Street are, of course, a dime a dozen, but their degrees were historically all in finance. My second and perhaps most significant qualification is that my MBA and most of my Wall Street background was in marketing. I studied consumer behavior—something totally absent in traditional finance curricula and completely foreign to the industry's mindset. When I began a somewhat unorthodox career path with E. F. Hutton & Co. in 1976, I'm sure I was one of very few marketing people on Wall Street at the time. At that time, there was no such thing as a marketing department or any kind of internal marketing organization.

Our biggest challenge at Hutton was to quickly launch new products in order to replace the revenue the firm was losing as clients moved to discount brokers. That ushered in a whirlwind era of new product launches such as cash-management accounts, tax shelters, listed options, managed futures accounts, and fee-based financial planning. To accomplish this, we did what marketing folks are supposed to do: we conducted primary market research to find out what our customers wanted (and, more importantly, what they were willing to pay for it). In the process, we were finding out for the very first time just what went on in the psyche of investors—what they knew, what they perceived, what they wanted from investing, and what they wanted from their brokers. It was quite an eye opener and totally virgin territory for a token marketing MBA in the investment world.

I discovered very early on that fundamental investment research was inadequate for developing a practical investment strategy, so I embraced the concept of technical analysis—a method of security analysis that relies on the assumption that market data can help predict future market trends. I studied price charts extensively throughout my investment career and spent a great deal of time utilizing methodologies such as Elliott wave analysis.

I have also been a licensed investment practitioner and have held management positions with financial institutions of one sort or another for the past 33 years, dealing with hundreds of brokers and thousands of individual clients. I've worked with portfolio managers, mutual funds, and option traders. As such, I've gained an extensive hands-on knowledge of the way people act with regard to investing, and thus began my journey into what is now being labeled behavioral finance.

## WHY SHARE?

This book will likely prompt some people to wonder why I did not use trend channel analysis to amass a huge amount of wealth before revealing it to the public. There are several answers to that. First, the book is not about a trading strategy or market anomaly that is so specific that it can no longer be effectively exploited once it has been shared with a great number of people. It is about a different way of thinking about the markets, and it can conceivably spawn any number of specific investment strategies and trading techniques, thereby allowing many people to benefit by it in different ways at the same time. It's also not a get-rich-quick scheme. It can enhance returns and help investors and traders move more efficiently through up-and-down cycles, but it's not a free lunch.

Second, as with all new market methods, the usual amount of skepticism will exist, and the resulting discussion and interpretation could easily go on for years. The landmark study by Brinson, Hood, and Beebower made public in 1971 concluded that the difference in investment performance among institutional investors was due mostly to sector allocation rather than individual stock picking. The study profoundly altered the thinking and behavior of professional investors and formed the basis for what later blossomed into modern portfolio theory. It took more than two decades for the professional investment community to fully embrace this thinking, and it is still unfamiliar to most individual investors. So while Lehman's trend channel hypothesis is debated in academic circles for several more decades, I'm hoping many of you will make good use of it in the meanwhile.

Third, withholding information such as this would offend my sense of academic advancement. At this point, I am content to share my revelations in the hope that others with additional insights and mathematical skills can further test, verify, refine, and enhance the theory for the betterment of all.

I chose to bring my work public through a book rather than as an academic article so that I can address it far more comprehensively and so that it can reach a much broader audience of investors as well as financial professionals. It is important to note that in its simplest form, the theory can be utilized by almost anyone with any size portfolio. It can be as useful to a long-term investor looking to position mutual funds in a 401(k) as it can be to a sophisticated short-term trader. The technique lends itself well to visually oriented analysis that is easy to understand and which I have been publicly sharing for several years through the StockCharts.com Website, where it is freely available.

# Introduction

## From Marketing to Market Trends: Epiphanies about Investor Behavior

PRIOR TO 1975, the word *marketing* was absent from Wall Street's vocabulary. On May 1st of that year, however, the brokerage world was forced into one of the quickest and most dramatic transformations in its history as the Securities and Exchange Commission (SEC) banned the fixed commission schedule previously imposed by the New York Stock Exchange (NYSE) on all member firms. The floodgates that held back discount brokerages opened almost immediately, and, for the first time, full-service Wall Street firms were forced to compete on price. Every major brokerage firm lost customers to the new discounters and was pressured to lower commissions for many of the customers who remained. The loss in revenue placed heavy pressure on the firms not only to develop alternate revenue sources from other services or products but also to seek (much to their own dismay) marketing help. As luck would have it, I graduated in May 1975 with a fresh marketing MBA and was looking for work in New York.

Wall Street firms jumped reluctantly into the world of marketing, opening a window for the first time into the minds of their customers. Shortly after fixed commissions were abolished, the NYSE, in a genuine but misguided attempt to help guide its member firms through this new marketing challenge, decided it would take on a leadership role as a market research entity. As a newly hired marketing manager at the NYSE, my first task was to analyze the data from a recently commissioned NYSE study, *Public Attitudes Toward Investing*—the largest study of its kind ever undertaken by the securities industry.

The research, conducted by the Princeton Research Institute, consisted of in-depth interviews with two thousand households. It probed the residents on their knowledge and attitudes toward investing, financial institutions, and a number of individual securities products. The data generated by that study filled reams of computer printouts from floor to ceiling. I was tasked with making sense of it and reporting the results to the exchange's member firms. It took more than a year and a team of several people, but what we learned about the investor mindset was as new to Wall Street as what scientists must have learned from the first rocks brought back from the moon.

To assist with the data analysis, I enlisted the help of a marketing professor, Dr. Thomas Stanley, from the State University of New York (SUNY) at Albany's graduate school of business, whose expertise was in the study of consumer behavior as it applied to banks and financial institutions. Tom later teamed up with SUNY finance professor William Danko to write the No. 1 bestseller *The Millionaire Next Door: The Surprising Secrets of America's Wealthy*. Tom is now considered one of the foremost experts in the world on how wealthy people think about things like money, banking, and investing.

We gave Tom an open mandate to examine the data with no preconceived hypotheses to prove or disprove. We would then determine what the implications of those results were for the securities industry. This approach maximized our objectivity with regard to the data. Tom conducted multivariate analysis on the data that showed sixteen separate market segments, all defined by *psychographic*, rather than demographic, characteristics. In other words, Wall Street's myopic view of the investor population stratifying by wealth was naïve. It was investors' goals, risk profiles, and attitudes about investing that distinguished them from their peers, not how much money they had. We summarized the results and made presentations to the senior execs at a number of Wall Street firms. There was enough raw data to keep a marketing department busy for the next decade.

Most of it, however, fell on deaf ears. Wall Street simply didn't have the marketing expertise to deal with it. In my mind, the revelation that investing could be analyzed like other types of consumer behavior is where behavioral finance *really* began—in 1978. Back then, however, we called it *financial marketing*, and no one in the industry paid any attention to it.

## The Waves of R. N. Elliott

While working at E. F. Hutton as an options liaison, I entered the U.S. Trading Championships to see how competitively I could trade options. To my own astonishment, I finished first among industry professionals in the option division and second in the overall championship. The nonprofessional who out-traded me was Robert Prechter, a former Merrill Lynch analyst who developed a theory linking investor mood swings to market action. Wall Street largely thought of him as a rogue. In the late 1970s, Prechter wrote a book and began publishing a newsletter on the wave principles of R. N. Elliott as they applied to the stock market. I introduced myself to Elliott wave analysis and immediately knew Prechter was on to something. Wall Street never took Prechter seriously, and the media only acknowledged him when his calls on the market were working, but Prechter went on to make what I consider a major fundamental contribution to a field he calls *socionomics* and that we now call *behavioral finance*.

Among other things, Elliott wave analysis steered me toward a focus on the markets, rather than on individual stocks, and I came to feel quite convinced that there were things going on at the market level that made it behave decidedly different from individual stocks. I also agreed with Prechter that there was a link between group sentiment and market action, though I felt something less ambiguous than R. N. Elliott's waves was needed for it to be used to develop practical investment strategy.

### New Insights

E. F. Hutton imploded in 1988 and became absorbed by rival Shearson. After various marketing roles, I took leave of the corporate world to start an option advisory service and to write *New Insights on Covered Call Writing* with Lawrence McMillan (Bloomberg Press, 2003). An overreaction to abusive option practices in the 1970s and 1980s led to a backlash against option trading of any kind by brokers and the general public. That led to a whole generation of investors as well as licensed brokers who didn't understand much about options at all much less that covered call writing is actually a conservative investment strategy. Meanwhile, advances in real-time quoting and execution made available through the Internet gave the public valuable trading tools for options and helped level the playing field with the professionals.

The strategy of covered call writing is a sound one, but the performance of portfolios strictly designed for covered call writing is highly dependent on picking the right stocks to begin with. Picking winners also requires picking a sufficient number of them to achieve diversification to protect against the unforeseen calamities that would eventually befall some of them. Stock research proved too burdensome for a one-man operation, and I shuddered at the idea of trying to do any better at it than professional analysts. Besides, fundamental research proved not to be effective. It didn't matter whether I did it myself or bought it from someone else. Furthermore, it was clear from the options activity I monitored that people in the know were routinely acting on both good and bad news on specific companies before it was made public—something I couldn't compete with.

The reality of covered call writing is that it works very well in flat, seesaw, or declining market periods but underperforms in strong up periods. I knew I could improve the strategy if I could reliably tell when the market was in an up, down, or sideways trend. Focusing again on the market as a whole, I realized that the overall market displayed more regular and predictable behavior than any individual stocks I followed. Stocks are subject to all manner of significant interruptions, anomalies, abnormal movements, and game playing by both inside executives and Wall Street analysts. Playing the options markets for years made these things all the more apparent. I reached the point where I could see things coming just by watching the options activity. The amount of advance option buying ahead of important not-yet-public announcements is staggering, and why this form of insider trading is allowed to continue so blatantly, I cannot fathom. Like so many other of Wall Street's transgressions over the years, this too will probably continue until it reaches a level that will be sufficiently heinous as to arouse the attention of someone whose career will benefit by its adjudication. The market, on the other hand, is relatively immune to the vagaries of individual stocks. It cannot announce an earnings surprise, be sued for product liability, or lie about its prospects.

When considering market movements, I began from scratch, drawing straight lines on charts I could now find online. The straight lines led to trend channels. Trend channels had promise but only explained some of the market's moves. Adding a few rules of my own creation fixed that problem. Now it became intriguing. The more I charted, the more times I saw a major index land dead on a previously drawn trend line and reverse. The accuracy of the channels amazed me. Days, weeks and sometimes even months later, an index would come back and perfectly touch a line drawn from prior peaks or troughs. While I was opening a totally new perspective on the market's behavior, an interesting phenomenon was occurring in the financial industry—the introduction of exchange-traded funds (ETFs).

As ETFs emerged on the broad market indexes and then expanded into industry sectors, emerging markets, and ultimately inverse index funds, they provided a myriad of ways to play market trends without needing to select individual stocks. Once options were introduced on many ETFs, I could then use options to fine-tune the strategy, hedge, or simply generate income through call writing. It was all starting to come together.

## THE TREND CHANNEL EPIPHANIES

As we all know, epiphanies are those "aha" moments when a swarm of previously unconnected nodes in your neural network suddenly link up to expose some kind of significant revelation. The cartoon depiction of an epiphany is the illumination of a giant lightbulb hovering over one's head. Two operative characteristics of epiphanies are that they are by nature instantaneous and they tend to turn previously intuitive notions upside-down. Mine held true to the latter but occurred in a more choppy fashion, with smaller epiphanies occurring over many years. I didn't even notice the lightbulb was lit until it had burned off most of my hair.

When ETFs arrived, I began tracking them by drawing simple trend lines connecting peaks and troughs on the price charts of major indexes like the Dow Jones Industrial Averages, Standard & Poor's

500 Index, and Nasdaq-100. The first epiphany was that parallel straight lines contain much of the market's zigs and zags in both short- and long-term time horizons. The second was that with a few intuitive modifications, they contained virtually *all* of the market's moves. The third was that trend lines worked extremely well on five-minute price charts, allowing for almost instantaneous recognition that the trend was changing or modifying itself. These were significant epiphanies, but the most important was yet to come.

There was inherent conflict between explaining the market's price behavior through technical analysis during the trading day and explaining it in terms of classic financial principles in the courses I taught at night. The two didn't mix. I began to read more and more about traditional finance in an effort to reconcile these opposing ideas. I read Malkiel's *A Random Walk Down Wall Street*. That led me to the books debunking the random walk and the related efficient market hypothesis, which began my descent into the maelstrom of what is now called behavioral finance. Ironically, the notion that investor psychology could affect the market's action connected me all the way back to the original revelations in investor psychology from the NYSE study in 1978 and to Prechter's wave analysis. It all came together—the studies, the weaknesses in classic finance, the charting, the behavioral work, and the realization that the charts were eloquently telling me what classic financial analysis could not: The stock market is not random after all; it is a function of the aggregate psychology and behavior of the participants and can be interpreted through an analysis of price charts, using techniques such as trend channel analysis. Furthermore, if not random, then the market is also, at least to some degree, *predictable!*

### THE BEHAVIORAL PERSPECTIVE

This book examines the stock market from a behavioral perspective, building on a growing body of content that views the action of the stock market not simply as a compilation of the actions of individual *stocks* but as the compilation of the actions of the *participants*. This perspective will add a new context to investment decision making that can make all of us better at tailoring our investment strategies. Such a perspective has been sorely missing in the industry and the media. The trend channel technique described in this book is a new way to interpret the behavior of the market and can be utilized to enhance existing investment strategies or formulate entirely new ones.

I offer this theory empirically, as a result of years of observation and technical analysis of the equity markets coupled with my knowledge as a thirty-year financial professional and as an instructor of both corporate finance and options. Skeptics may claim that my technique is unproven as a means of managing investments. You can decide for yourself whether my hypothesis has merit or whether you want to wait twenty years for the theory to be fully accepted by the investment community.

For all intents and purposes, virtually all of the research in behavioral finance has thus far been conducted by the academic community. While a valuable body of work has been amassed, much of it suffers from a lack of practical trading and investing knowledge. Richard Thaler, a Cornell professor who compiled a number of behavioral finance papers into *Advances in Behavioral Science* (The Russell Sage Foundation, 1993) and *Advances in Behavioral Finance Volume II* (The Russell Sage Foundation, 2005), admits that a great many papers on behavioral finance have been written by recent doctoral graduates and that their lack of industry experience tends to show up in their assumptions as well as conclusions. Most important, while the fact that behavior affects stock prices has been convincingly demonstrated, little has been drawn from these findings to alter investment strategy. We may know more, but we have yet to meaningfully incorporate that knowledge into the practice of investment management.

While my trend channel observations occasionally yield moments of astonishing accuracy in predicting market movement, there are occasions that fall short of expectations and others that prove later to be false signals. Frequently, the observations require interpretive judgment. As such, this analysis is not in any way presented as a crystal ball or as a formula for calling every top and bottom with perfect accuracy. However, it need only provide an edge to be a highly useful and effective tool. A blackjack player doesn't need to know the order of the deck to beat the house. He just needs to have enough knowledge to put the probabilities slightly in his favor. The same is true for investors and traders.

## WHAT TO EXPECT

Given the mind-numbing battery of books available on financial matters, here's what you can expect from this book:

- A compelling argument that the stock market is not entirely random—as we have been so often led to believe—but instead behaves in characteristic ways that can be explained within certain parameters.
- An easy-to-follow charting technique that can give anyone the ability to get a visual perspective on what the market is "doing" at any point in time and in the context of almost any time period.
- A methodology for determining when a market trend has indeed changed and when the direction has changed within a longer trend.
- A way to make at least some sense out of seemingly chaotic or extreme market moves.
- A context in which to make or time investment decisions.
- The tools to develop a trading strategy that could significantly enhance overall investment returns, regardless of market conditions.

This book is not written only for traders, though it contains all the elements needed to develop a number of different trading methodologies. It is not written only for academics, though it will provoke much in the way of ideas for further study and analysis. It is not written only for investment professionals, though it will expand their perspective beyond that which was ingrained in them by the industry. It is written for anyone who invests in the market, regardless of profession, trading expertise, or academic level.

# PART I

## A Market of What?

# The Time Has Come 1

> *"The time has come," the Walrus said, "to talk of many things: of shoes and ships and sealing wax, of cabbages and kings."*
>
> LEWIS CARROLL
> *Through the Looking-Glass*

THE TIME HAS come to stop listening to the party line from Wall Street and the academic community and to stop deluding ourselves about the stock market. We need to accept the market for what it really is and embrace a new perspective about why the market behaves the way it does. Then we need to seriously adjust our investment tactics accordingly.

Both the investment industry and the academic community have for too long defended a stock market paradigm conceived in a different age and based on theoretical concepts that have been questioned time and time again. The inner workings of the investment world are as different as they could possibly be from the days when much of the current principles of corporate finance and investment management were developed more than a half century ago. New insights on the market have arisen but have not yet been widely disseminated.

In the tumult surrounding the crash of 1929 and the subsequent Great Depression, there were sweeping changes in how the public looked at stocks. Congress produced a flurry of legislation in the 1930s and 1940s designed to regulate the industry and protect investors from the kind of unscrupulous practices that were blamed for much of the damage that had taken place during that catastrophe.

Financial academia went into high gear searching for answers and attempting to place a more rational spin on the behavior of the financial markets. Most of the resulting intellectual framework that was built during this period is still intact today.

Yet we all know how dramatically different things are today from the 1920s and 1930s. On those fateful trading days at the end of October 1929, the total volume on the New York Stock Exchange was around ten million shares. Today, a ten-million-share day is routine for a single actively traded stock! In addition to the expansive increase in the number of stocks and shares traded, the very nature of the financial marketplace has been altered by technologies that enable millions of people to trade from their own computers and by a reshaping of the market as a truly global phenomenon. But the basic thinking that underlies how we view the movements of the stock market hasn't changed much. It has merely been broadened to accommodate all the financial events that have occurred since: the go-go years of the 1950s and 1960s, the crash of 1987, the Internet bubble of the 1990s, and everything else that the markets have experienced.

It is time to talk of many things: things that have been alluded to by many prominent people during the last century but not pursued in earnest; things the financial industry practices but won't acknowledge; things that are anathema to financial academia; human things. We need to see the stock market for what it is: a market not of stocks, but of people, and thus driven by human behavior as much (if not more so) than financial or economic factors. Doing so will grant us greater clarity about the nature and direction of the market, and thus we will become far more effective participants. For those who seek more than just financial enlightenment, there is also the potential to dramatically improve overall returns from equity investments.

Calling into question decades-old dogma about what moves the stock market may generate a healthy skepticism. Let me bolster the case by relating that much of what's in this book comes from people in the industry or in academia who have already planted the seeds of new thinking about the stock market. There is now a groundswell of work from a small but growing number of highly regarded authors, academics, and financial professionals surrounding the behavioral view of the market. I am helping to carry the message further, adding additional insights, and providing practical advice on using this new information. Nonetheless, there is substantial resistance for this idea from the mainline financial industry and from much of the old guard. Changing a nearly century-old paradigm in thinking isn't a simple matter. Changing the way the investment industry works and the way investors think is even more difficult.

To accept what is put forth in this book, you will need to open your mind to a different perspective about what the stock market is all about and why it behaves the way it does. That is not to say that I recommend throwing conventional financial principles out the window and relying instead on reading tea leaves or consulting the constellations. It means adding an important piece of legitimate analysis that has, until now, been largely absent from the accepted wisdom in both the academic world and on Wall Street. To appreciate the value of this missing piece, you will need to immunize yourself from the barrage of information you are exposed to about the financial markets and accept some concepts that are avidly rejected by many industry professionals. In addition, you'll need to accept that the teachings of most academic institutions and financial certification programs may be comprehensive and well reasoned but seriously one-sided.

If you are willing to take this leap, you will be supported by a growing body of research and the writings of numerous practitioners and academics. You will be presented with a new tool that will facilitate your investment decisions, free you of the need to rely on investment research on individual stocks, and allow you to achieve better returns than what most professionals offer. At the very least, this book will expand your perspective on stock investing and make it less complicated. For some of you, it may free you of the need to pay an investment advisor; for others who already self-manage, it may enable you to implement a much more rewarding investment plan than anything you have had in the past. For those who fully embrace the new order of stock investing, dramatic improvements in returns and reductions in risk are possible.

## MISINFORMATION AT THE SPEED OF LIGHT

The stock market could well be the most widely misunderstood, misinterpreted, and misperceived phenomenon in America. That's not an off-the-cuff remark. Personal and professional experience over thirty years, including teaching at both the college and professional level, has confirmed that fact over and over again, not just across the average working population, but among highly educated individuals and even among financial industry professionals.

Don't confuse information with comprehension. Technology has graced us with access to magnitudes more information today about stocks and the markets than ever before. But the irony of the Internet's blessings and curses are readily apparent. Despite the tremendous advances in real-time online news, information, and trading, most people appear no closer to understanding how the stock market behaves than when the information was only available in the newspaper. Information is plentiful, but comprehension sorely lags. While a minority of people have benefited considerably from the improvements in information technology, many are overwhelmed by it; surprisingly, the chasm between the information haves and the information have-nots has effectively widened.

Indeed, the information pendulum has now swung all the way from dearth to excess. Studies clearly prove that too much information actually hinders decision making. Today, a mass of opinionated commentary pervades the media, information from noncredible or nonobjective sources abounds, and tons of misleading information are disseminated by third parties for self-serving purposes. (Did you know, for example, that you can legally pay a third party who has no financial credentials whatsoever and has done no research on your business, to publish glowing remarks about your company as long as they indicate in the fine print that they were paid to do so?) Separating well-reasoned financial interpretations from naïve, uneducated guesses or self-serving promotions can be daunting, particularly when those pronouncements emanate from sources we trust to be credible.

In addition, the movement toward "Web 2.0" is taking information in the direction of garnering more and more content from the audience itself. With blogs and other ways to self-publish rapidly expanding, you could find yourself reading financial comments from a 7-year-old, an incarcerated felon, or a jilted employee exacting revenge on a former employer. The only credential necessary to offer a financial opinion in mass media these days is a computer.

Frustration over the market's volatility and seemingly inconsistent meanderings commonly breeds illusions by many people that the markets are fixed—conveniently manipulated by the big firms, the traders, the short sellers, the hedge funds, the banks, or worse ... the U.S. government. Sadly, I find more of this kind of speculation from professionals than from individual investors, and it causes me to wonder which scenario is worse—that they're wrong or that they might be right.

Adding to this awkward scenario is the perverse state of regulation in our country that permits unscrupulous people outside the industry to say whatever they please while muzzling the very professionals inside the industry who we would hope to be more knowledgeable and better informed. Anything that can be construed as a recommendation from a licensed professional has to have so many reviews and caveats heaped on it that the entire communication process frequently caves in under its own weight. In addition, financial institutions have long since determined that the less they tell or teach their constituents, the safer they are from lawsuits that challenge their message or claim that it was not uniformly communicated to their entire audience. Similarly, corporate officials have retreated under the harsh potential liabilities of Sarbanes-Oxley legislation. Meanwhile, unlicensed armchair market know-it-alls can run amok with communications that are unchecked, unverified, and wholly unsubstantiated.

What's particularly disturbing about the financial industry is that so many brokers believe they are experts at managing money simply by virtue of having passed the securities licensing exam—which, by the way, is largely about rules and regulations and has strikingly few questions on how to manage a client's portfolio or what makes a good investment. Those with enhanced credentials like certified financial planner and certified financial analyst are considerably better grounded in financial principles but no less prone to making judgments based on their own beliefs or emotions.

Perhaps one of the biggest flaws in our financial structure is the fact that with precious few exceptions, investment professionals are paid to collect assets or to sell us products and not for the performance of our portfolios. Bluntly, they are both trained and incentivised in sales—not investment management. As Alan Abelson of *Barron's* eloquently stated, "Selling, not analysis, has always been Wall Street's strong suit, as even a cursory review of its record as a seer, whether of market trends or of particular stocks, will readily confirm."[1] So while they naturally benefit by having our assets remain with them (and they do realize a slightly greater fee each year when these assets appreciate), they have little other concern for how well our investments actually perform, except to make sure that they perform roughly in line with everyone else in order to keep us from taking our assets to one of their competitors. In many instances, financial advisors are compensated not just for getting you into an investment but also throughout the life of that investment, even though they won't likely have any impact on it (or any communication with you about it) once they've placed you in it.

Like it or not, we're almost all in the great stock game in one way or another. If you don't own stocks directly, then your mutual fund, insurance company, college endowment, or retirement plan certainly does. There's no getting away from it. The bottom line is that trillions of dollars are entrusted by individuals to investment professionals, many of whom have inadequate training and no direct incentives to make money for their clients. They are also saddled with the administrative burden of dealing with a large number of accounts and a huge amount of regulatory overhead governing their every word and action. So it becomes imperative to find a common approach they can utilize for most or all of their clients. You may think your advisor is constantly looking out for your account, but most of the time he or she has given the management of your account to someone else while they look for more assets to manage.

## THE "OTHER" ANALYSIS

Fundamental financial analysis, the tried and true methodology for valuing stocks, uses variables such as earnings expectations, price multiples, present values, and risk premiums, among other factors, to determine the underlying or intrinsic value of a stock. As logical and scientifically well grounded as this type of analysis is, the simple truth is that by itself, fundamentals can be horribly ineffective at determining or justifying actual stock prices. At best, they provide a guideline for where stocks or the market as a whole theoretically should be, but it is market forces (i.e., the whims of the participants) at any particular moment that determine the actual market price of any stock. And those whims are brought about by a myriad of behavioral variables that frequently have little or nothing to do with the variables used by fundamental analysts.

In addition, fundamental analysis itself is not an exact science. (If it were, all the analysts would come up with the same results and we would need a whole lot fewer of them!) Forward-looking estimates and a slew of assumptions are required to arrive at an earnings estimate or a stock recommendation. Among different analysts at different firms, one can frequently see a wide disparity in fundamental interpretation among them, even on the same companies. Even the analysts themselves acknowledge that the fundamentally determined price of a stock is a moving target and that the market at any particular moment may price a stock radically differently.

The problem is that the difference between equation-produced price estimates and actual market prices for stocks can persist for a very long time and simply cannot be explained by fundamental analysis. Consequently, we are taught that we have to just accept these differences and that for stocks held over a long enough period of time, the differences will tend to cancel themselves out in favor of a long-term trend that will exhibit an upward bias due to inflation, compounded earnings, and other factors.

The entire investment business thus revolves around tenets of fundamental analysis that are essentially lousy at explaining the reality of stock prices. What's more, they can be lousy by a huge and unpredictable margin. Even more bothersome is the fact that fundamental analysis does almost nothing for valuing the market as a whole. At best it gives us vague limits of earnings multiples on the market based on historic averages. (Much more on fundamental analysis in Chapter 2.)

Meanwhile, stocks move extensively over the course of a given year in ways that cannot be explained by changes in fundamentals. In 2006, for example, the Dow Jones Industrial Average rose 16.3 percent—an above-average year by historic standards. The total absolute value of daily movements in the index for the same year, however, was 115.5 percent. That means that in order to achieve that 16.3-percent return over the course of the year, one had to ride a roller coaster up and down for a total of nearly eight times that amount. In 2007, the same index was up a paltry 6.4 percent while the daily price swings totaled 164.4 percent—more than twenty-five times the annual return. In 2008, hanging on for the entire year one suffered a loss of 33.8 percent, with daily swings adding up to 412.2 percent! This is what buy-and-hold investors experience year after year.

There is, however, another type of analysis on which some investors rely that embraces price swings rather than ignoring them. It's called *technical analysis* (TA), and while it is given only minimal credence by Wall Street, I (and many others) feel it is the vitally missing ingredient to stock market interpretation. If you buy the concept that behavioral factors are what causes price swings, then TA is the way to incorporate the behavioral factors into your investment strategy.

Technical analysis may represent voodoo to fundamental purists, but it is widely and religiously practiced by traders of all types, both professional and nonprofessional. A huge number of books have been written on the subject, and a substantial number of people practice it, whether by itself or in combination with some kind of fundamental analysis. Indeed, even the trading departments of major brokerages keep an eye on the charts, though they would never ever make a stock recommendation to clients on that basis.

While I am a devoted advocate of technical analysis, I will readily admit that I do not necessarily ascribe to all types of TA available. In fact, I had to develop a modified version of one technique in particular before becoming totally sold on its value. The fact that there is little support for the technique among academics leaves lots of things to interpretation or simply to be defined by the users themselves. Nevertheless, technical analysis is the only tool we currently have for incorporating behavioral analysis into the stock market at the aggregate level.

## Trend Channels

In this book, I detail the use of a specific aspect of technical analysis known as *trend channel analysis*. None of the other indicators by themselves have been as effective for me as the channels, though other technical indicators used with the trend channels do offer even more effective implementation. It is important to note that trend channels appear to be affected by behavioral influences and may offer one of the few ways we can gain insights on the behavioral aspects of the stock market.

Very few people have been devotees of trend channels as they simply haven't provided continuity, accuracy, or reliability in the past. Once I modified the technique, I began to observe market movements that fit into channels with uncanny precision—far too much to just be coincidence. Since then I have been exclusively using the channels for market analysis and have published my interpretations freely on the Internet (in the "Public chart lists" section at www.StockCharts.com). I continue to receive e-mail from people around the world who comment about how simple and intuitive the technique is and how much more effective they have been in their investing as a result.

## Hidden in Plain Sight

The following example illustrates how the use of a trend channel offers investors a new perspective on the stock market. On January 3, 2005, the Standard & Poor's 500 Index (SPX) hit an intraday high of 1217.90. Two and a half years later on July 18, 2007, the SPX hit an intraday high of 1555.24 (see **FIGURE 1.1**). A straight line drawn between these two points on a logarithmic graph of SPX daily prices contains all of the SPX's daily price moves for that thirty-month period. The line just happens, by the way, to be rising at a rate of close to 10 percent per year, approximating the average long-term annualized return of the stock market.

By drawing a similar line connecting the two lowest points during that same interval, we would connect the intraday low of 1228.45 on July 18, 2006, with the intraday low of 1406.10 on November 26, 2007. Together, these two lines form what is called a *trend channel*: two boundary lines that contain virtually all the daily price movements of an index, equity, or other security for a given time period.

Once drawn, the two lines appear to be roughly parallel. That perception is supported mathematically by the fact that the two lines are 99 percent correlated. This is significant, since the accepted wisdom is that stock prices follow a so-called random walk. If that were the case, then it would be mighty coincidental that these two lines turned out to be so perfectly parallel. So I enlisted a statistics major at Berkeley to help run some tests, and we generated 100,000 simulations of data similar to this series. The tests showed that a data series like this would result in the two highest and two lowest points lying on parallel lines about 1.5 percent of the time if the data was truly random. Said another way, we could be confident that this was *not* a random occurrence. This fact has enormous implications for predicting stock prices.

There's more. A third high on August 16, 2007, also precisely hit the upper line, and a third low on June 1, 2007, precisely hit the lower line. Six points, months apart from one another, out of more than 270 daily price movements, all touched two perfectly parallel trend lines—not over the line by even a little bit, but with pinpoint accuracy. The odds of that being a coincidence are infinitesimal. So is the market truly random? Far from it.

Now, given the long-term average annual 10-percent rise in the market, this data set is representative of "normal" or expected performance. But remember that the index is traversing this channel over time. So if you bought in January 2005 and held until July 2007, you would have indeed realized a 27.6 percent gain (about 11 percent on an annualized basis). But for the nineteen months between January 2005 and July 2006, the index was almost totally flat; and had you entered the market in January 2005 but sold one month later than July 2007, you would have achieved a total gain of about 13 percent for the thirty-one months (about 5 percent annualized).

Figure 1.1    SPX 2005–2007

Source: StockCharts.com

The point is that the overall trend of the channel did as would be expected over the long term, but the distance between the lower and upper boundary of the channel was about 200 points or about 14 percent of the index. Thus, if you bought at the high end of the trend channel, your best scenario over that period was 11 percent per year, and your worst was around 5 percent per year. Even in the best scenario, you had to put up with internal trend fluctuations of up to 14 percent several times to make 11 percent per year. Clearly, buying near the lower channel boundary and selling near the higher one would have made a big difference in your performance. What's more, buying at the wrong time can lose you money, even in a rising trend! On the other hand, had you bought at 1225 in July 2006 and sold at the first touch of the upper line in June 2007, you would have realized more than 25 percent in less than one year.

Naturally, we can postulate all we want with 20/20 hindsight. However, if the lines above could have been drawn months before the upper and lower touch points in late 2007 actually occurred, then I should think we would all have found that advantageous. The fact is they were. The acceptance of behavioral influences on stock prices will catapult us into a whole new perspective on investing, and the use of trend channel analysis can help us incorporate this new perspective into our investment strategy.

## WHAT THE MARKET IS TELLING US

Investors of all types have felt the effects of the market tumult of 2008–2009, and for many it represented a devastating blow, not just to their wealth but to their confidence in the conventional buy-and-hold wisdom. Individuals and professionals alike will attempt to extract lessons from this experience.

At a practical level, the market is telling investors that reliance on the conventional wisdom about stock investing may not be in their best interest. But how then are they to view the market? Behavioral finance begins to answer that question. We are wired for emotions like greed, anticipation, fear, and a host of others that affect our purchase behavior. We may be different from one another, but as professional marketers and advertisers know, we can be grouped together in ways that our collective behavior can be not only characterized but also predicted. In other words, investing in stocks can be looked at as just another form of consumer behavior.

Most important, however, the market may be able to tell us where it is going. For that, we need tools that can interpret the market in different terms than the fundamental economic terms currently employed by most professionals. That is where technical analysis in general and trend channel analysis in particular are best applied.

The thrust of this book is to explore what the market is telling us from these different perspectives. Accordingly, the remainder of Part I exposes the flaws in conventional stock market thinking and valuation, Part II explores the new behavioral view of the markets, and Part III offers one of the first practical tools for incorporating the new perspective into investment strategy.

### CHAPTER NOTE

1. Alan Abelson, "The Not-So-Great Depression," *Barron's*, February 27, 2009.

# Fundamentally Flawed   *2*

*I am no longer an advocate of elaborate techniques of security analysis in order to find superior value opportunities.*[1]

BENJAMIN GRAHAM

THE CENTRAL PILLAR supporting Wall Street's expertise is financial analysis. Corporate financial analysis enables investment bankers to garner exorbitant fees for advising companies on debt or equity issuance, helping them evaluate strategic options like buybacks or going private, and bringing new securities to market. Financial analysis applied to product development powers the manufacturing process for thousands of derivatives, unit trusts, limited partnerships, exchange-traded funds, and other securities products designed to satisfy every conceivable niche in the financial marketplace. And it is a repackaged form of financial analysis that we have come to know as *fundamental stock research*—analysts' recommendations on individual stocks—that provides so-called full-service firms with a justification for charging substantially more to execute a stock trade than discount brokers.

Few people question Wall Street's financial expertise. The industry buys a fresh crop of new MBAs each year and allies itself with the top business schools in financial research. Its methodologies are built on widely accepted, well-honed principles of finance that have been used for decades and have been sanctioned by all the appropriate regulatory bodies and accounting organizations. It is important to note that their research has also withstood enough legal battles over the years to enable its continued dissemination, albeit accompanied by the necessary caveats, exclusions, and disclaimers. Few people would deny the necessity of having an ongoing analysis on the overall economy and conducting basic research on industry sectors, individual companies, and now even on investment opportunities in other countries in support of managing their investments. But it can easily be argued that securities firms cannot effectively avoid the inherent conflicts of interest in rating the very products they sell. Even more important, fundamental research fails to explain completely the ongoing behavior of stocks and is thus inadequate as a sole methodology for picking stocks or knowing when to buy or sell them.

From a financial perspective, fundamental research is certainly credible, even though it is not always an exact science. It is rooted in widely accepted principles such as the time value of money, discounted cash flows, and risk versus return. Analysts are highly trained and paid huge salaries for their work. For that, they are expected not just to crank out the numbers but also to produce value-added insight and judgment about what's behind the numbers and where things are going, as well as to take a more objective view of them than we might receive from the company's own executives. But the simple reality is that corporate fundamentals provide little more than a guide for assessing the value of common stock—one that is subsequently interpreted and assessed by the investing public and thousands of investment professionals. As a result of the human overlay, it becomes nothing more than a rough benchmark for stock pricing and doesn't fully explain why stocks behave the way they do. Analysts themselves will readily point out that it is not expected to explain short-term price movements in stocks or support short-term trading. But even from a long-term investing perspective, fundamental analysis doesn't offer a way of creating and managing a portfolio that will outperform the benchmark averages either.

Why is fundamental analysis flawed? Why do stocks vary so much in value when the fundamentals don't change that often? And why does the industry rely so heavily on fundamentals when they work so poorly? This chapter addresses these questions.

## TRADITIONALISM

Traditionalism is one of the hallmarks of Wall Street—wing-tip shoes, pin-striped suits, leather wingback chairs. I recall one executive at E. F. Hutton who had been promoted to senior vice president and moved to the New York headquarters from Connecticut. His new office in Battery Park was palatial and decked with paintings of hunting scenes. Figuring he had now made it high enough in the organization to decide for himself how to decorate his office, he had the hunting scenes removed and replaced them with sailing scenes. Within a few months, he was back in Connecticut and the hunting scenes were back on the wall in Battery Park.

Traditional thinking on Wall Street is no more apparent anywhere than in the way companies and stocks are analyzed. Analysts follow the tried and true methods that have been taught in finance classes for most of the last century and utilize them in practice with the religious dedication of Tibetan monks. They analyze a company's business lines—costs, revenues, trends, new products or locations, competitive factors, and so on. They take its complete financial measurements—book value, capital structure, various financial ratios—and compare them to benchmarks. Then they determine the projected net income that the overall business will produce and arrive at a value for the stock accordingly. This is grossly oversimplified, but the point is that fundamental research examines a company in just about every financial way possible, but only in financial terms.

Fundamental research is important, but even the analysts who produce it know that it is not capable of pegging stock prices or timing investment decisions. Benjamin Graham, one of the originators of some of the techniques used today, admitted in the quote above that, after many years, he no longer felt confident in the lengthy process of securities analysis that he himself helped develop. But analysts continue to use the traditional methods, and brokerage firms continue to tout their research, comforted by the fact that no one has yet to come up with a method that is considered to be better than fundamental analysis, so their results are essentially the best there is.

### VARIOUS SHADES OF BUY

Like so many other first-time investors, I entered the financial world naïvely believing that research analysts held the keys to the kingdom of stock market riches. After all, who other than a professional research analyst with a thorough knowledge of finance, a deep familiarity with the industry, and an inside track to the company's top officers could better divine a stock's current value or future potential? I even fell prey to my employer's famous advertising slogan, "When E. F. Hutton talks, people listen."

The first thing that struck me as odd was that once I bought something, there was no such thing as a *sell* recommendation. Ratings were almost all couched in various shades of *buy* (not unlike the way soft drinks at fast-food restaurants are now sold in various shades of large) and remained that way indefinitely. It soon became obvious that brokers were virtually always in buy mode, recommending that a stock be sold only on those rare occasions when it sold off so much that the firm needed to issue a *sell* just to save face (and, no doubt, so that they could defend themselves against possible legal action).

The phenomenon hasn't changed much even today. On Friday, September 12, 2008, the news was painted with headlines that described dire straits for Lehman Brothers Holdings, Inc. (LEH). Lehman's stock closed at 3.65, down from a price of 20 one month prior, 45 four months prior, and 65 seven months prior. Desperate weekend meetings with U.S. Treasury Department officials and possible suitors were being held in attempts to keep the firm from going under. Checking the *Wall Street Journal*'s research summary on LEH the night of the 12th, I found the following:

Ratings for LEH[2]

| Rating | No. Analysts |
|---|---|
| Strong Buy | 1 |
| Buy | 1 |
| Hold | 16 |
| Underperform | 0 |
| Sell | 0 |
| **Total surveyed** | 18 |

Price targets for the stock ranged from 9 to 71, and the overall rating of the stock by 18 analysts stood at 2.79. That equates to an overall rating somewhere between a "hold" and a "buy." Most startling of all was the fact that the current overall rating was *higher than the ratings of each of the prior three months*. The stock was down 90 percent in value over the prior three months, the entire world knew the company was on the ropes, there wasn't a single underperform or sell recommendation on the Street, and the analysts' ratings were going up!

For a time I worked at the venerable New York Stock Exchange. People there didn't bother to whisper when they passed information around on stocks. I was at a meeting with a high-ranking executive one day when his phone rang. I could tell from the conversation that it was from one of the specialists on the floor. By itself, that was not unusual, as the exec would normally be called if anything on the trading floor required his attention. The exec echoed enough of the conversation for me to realize that they were talking about the action on one of the stocks trading on the exchange floor a few stories below. The exec asked, "Should I get out now?" He got his answer, thanked the specialist, and excused himself to me while he called his broker and sold 2,000 shares. I guess there are some places on Wall Street where sell recommendations actually do exist.

Brokerage firms are virtually always in accumulation mode where the public is concerned. It's ingrained in their training and everyday mentality. They have convinced their clients and themselves that the market always goes up in the long run, and that no one can forecast the next move, so the only thing to do is to buy in now and get on the train before it leaves the station. It's never a question of whether you should buy a stock now or later—it's only a question of *which* stock to buy. Wall Street doesn't believe in timing the market, and no one there has a methodology for doing that. They cannot tell you whether today, tomorrow, or next month is a better time to buy. (There's a chapter on market timing later in the book.) They believe that the market always goes up "in the long term" and therefore if you buy in now you will eventually be rewarded. Meanwhile, had you bought into the market in the beginning of 2000, you would have been at zero gain six years later at the beginning of 2006 and again at the end of 2008. Does the "long-term" argument make you want to run out and buy a few stocks today?

Brokerage firms, like airplanes, are built to go in only one direction. They only have a forward gear, because they only have a method of picking stocks—not for telling when it's a good time to buy or sell them. Even if they did have a method of determining when to get in and out of stocks, the sheer responsibility of making all those precise buy and sell timing decisions for tens of thousands of clients who all bought in at different prices would be impossible to manage. In fact, that's a big reason why issuing sell recommendations is problematic.

Another reason why so many stocks are buys is because many of them are companies with which your brokerage firm has an investment banking (IB) relationship. Until I knew otherwise, I was quite impressed with how E. F. Hutton seemed to have IB relationships with so many companies whose stocks were so highly recommended. I figured the firm was just an elitist banker and that only the best private companies came to Hutton to be brought public. Later, I actually worked on an initial public offering (IPO) and saw how the system worked. The commitment to provide ongoing research is part of the agreement to bring the company public, and a positive recommendation is all but assured, not just for the IPO, but on a continuing basis thereafter. The broker also benefits from positive research as it helps sell the IPO and keep up an ongoing interest in the stock. In essence, the research was more of a marketing tool than objective commentary. Brokers used it to coax orders from institutional and retail clients. The better the deal went and the more demand that followed to pump up the stock, the more of a success the process was. That (and the intentional pricing of IPOs at very conservative levels) would pretty much ensure a deal's success and foster lots of interest in the next deal and the one after that. It was all so obviously self-serving.

All of this, of course, is well documented old news. In 2001, columnist Ben Cole authored an exposé on Wall Street analysts titled *The Pied Pipers of Wall Street,* in which he said, "The law and current regulation don't recognize what almost every Wall Street pro no longer even considers controversial: that Wall Street today is a half century and a world away from the business climate embodied in SEC regulations. Where once independence was their hallmark, analysts today are effectively part of the investment banking and marketing departments of brokerages."[3]

As a postscript to the analyst story, the practice of intentionally putting a positive spin on companies with which firms have an investment banking relationship was widespread across Wall Street and persisted until finally brought to light by New York Attorney General Elliot Spitzer and settled in 2003 through the payment of $875 million by the ten largest offenders.[4] So, the offenders got their hands slapped because they had made the practice a little too blatant and because they pressured analysts a little too much, but nothing structurally changed to reduce or eliminate the positive bias that will always exist on research for companies that have investment banking relationships.

Even more revealing in those early days was the fact that research, while based on sound and highly detailed fundamental analysis, seemed to have little bearing whatsoever on the price movements in the stock, except perhaps to explain why a stock had *already* had a healthy rise. That actually made sense when you considered that by the time the research was made public, it could have been weeks in the making, and that analysts at other firms would have already issued positive reports as well. What finally drove the point home for me was a conversation held while riding home on the train with a neighbor who worked for the same firm in institutional sales. I had seen some research come out earlier that day and asked him if he'd seen it for his institutional clients. He said, "Of course, we've been buying it for institutions for more than a week now." Discovering that the firm's institutional clients were given the same research days before it was disseminated to individual clients was the final straw for me. I never again relied on published research to make an investment decision.

## Can You Really Compare Today with the 1930s?

A little history helps to put fundamental research in perspective. As with much of the legal and regulatory infrastructure for the financial industry, the basics of how analysts evaluate stocks date back to the post-crash era of the 1930s. Benjamin Graham, a professor at Columbia Business School, was himself nearly wiped out in the crash of 1929. In its aftermath, he set out to develop a sensible technique for establishing the fair value of a stock. He enlisted David LeFevre Dodd, a recent PhD and assistant professor also at Columbia, and in 1934 they published a book called *Security Analysis*. Graham and Dodd offered a methodology for evaluating the financial merits of stocks and suggested a particular set of criteria for identifying undervalued stocks. The book remains one of the fixtures of American financial rhetoric, and seventy-five years later, it is still used as a textbook at Columbia.

It is difficult today to imagine what information flow was like in the 1920s and 1930s compared to now. The lack of reliable information coupled with the slow speed of dissemination no doubt contributed to the frothy stock market of the 1920s, the substantial number of scams and manipulations of the day, and the subsequent market collapse in the 1930s. In the aftermath of the great crash of 1929, Graham and Dodd set out to adopt a formal approach to valuing companies—ostensibly, one that would place realistic valuations on them so as to prevent egregious overpaying, which produces increased risk and might ultimately lead to another crash. Their technique advocated finding stocks that had a low price-to-earnings ratio (P/E) relative to its own P/E history, a high dividend yield, and a market price below its book value. They also wanted to see total debt less than book value, a current ratio greater than two, earnings growth of at least 7 percent over the prior ten years, and no more than a 5-percent decline in earnings in more than two of those ten years.

Remember that these criteria come on the heels of a market environment that compares to present-day markets like the horse-drawn buggy compares to a computer-enhanced, precision-engineered, navigationally equipped automobile. They were deliberately conservative and conceived in the aftermath of the wild valuations that led to the great crash. While some people point to the success of Warren Buffett, a well-known Graham and Dodd disciple, as proof the technique works, evidence from the authors themselves suggests otherwise. The annual returns of the Graham Joint Account between 1925 and 1935 averaged 6 percent annually versus the Standard & Poor's 500 Index at 5.8 percent, and the returns of the Graham-Newman Corp. for 1945 to 1956 averaged 15.3 percent versus 18.3 percent for the S&P during that period. While the Graham technique did have less volatility, the returns were less than stellar for all the work that would have gone into the analysis. In the 1940 edition of their book, Graham and Dodd admit, "Our search for definite investment standards for the common-stock buyer has been more productive of warning than of concrete suggestions. We have been led to the old principle that the investor should wait for periods of depressed business and market levels to buy representative common stocks, since he is unlikely to be able to acquire them at other times except at prices that the future may require him to regret."[5] This is a profound statement about the merits of using fundamental analysis as the sole criteria for investing in stocks made by two of the most important figures in the development of the technique.

The securities markets, the players, and the trading tools of today are worlds different than in the 1930s. News and information reaches millions of people instantaneously. Trades execute in fractions of a second. Trading volume on an average day is now a thousand times what it was then. It is a gross understatement to say that it's a very different world today. Meanwhile, despite the problems of relying entirely on fundamental analysis, an army of professional analysts and many private and institutional investors still engage in the technique on a regular basis—to the exclusion of almost any other methodology.

### INTRINSIC VALUE: THE FINANCIAL GRAIL

The ultimate objective of fundamental research is to determine the investment merit of a stock. It does this by attempting to calculate its fair or *intrinsic* value, which is determined by its future prospects at generating profits. In theory, armed with an intrinsic value, a firm or investment manager could recommend a stock for purchase when its current market price is sufficiently below that or recommend selling the stock if the market price is sufficiently above it. Supposedly, the firm or manager can uncover opportunities for attractive gains where the future prospects of a stock are not being properly valued in today's prices. Reality, as you already know, is far different from this scenario.

Ideally, an intrinsic value for a stock might function like the published book value for used cars pioneered by Les Kelley. The folks at Kelley Blue Book take the price of a new car and depreciate it throughout the useful life of a car to determine guidelines for what that car should be worth each year of its life. They even account for the approximate mileage and condition of the car and the various options you could have on it. The book values published by Kelley are now widely available on the Internet, so when you are looking to buy or sell a used car, you can obtain a very good idea of what the price should be. You may pay more or less in reality, depending on things like availability, proximity, and local supply and demand. When gas hit $4.50 per gallon, a used Prius would sell for more than book value, while a Yukon would sell for less. Intrinsic values for stocks, even though far more complex and variable than the book value for a car, would serve a similar function—that is, if we had them.

But we don't. No one does. Intrinsic values for stocks are a purely theoretical concept. There is no way you can look one up, and no way to know whether any price represented to you by an analyst actually *is* the intrinsic value at any point in time. In fact, you won't even get the same intrinsic value from multiple analysts due to the different methodologies and assumptions involved in the calculations. You can go through the motions of determining what you think is an intrinsic value, but do not expect that the value you arrive at will be anywhere near an absolute.

The idea behind fundamental analysis and intrinsic value is logical enough, and absent anything else, it is easy to become overreliant on both. One analyzes a company's current business and examines its financial prospects, risks, and opportunities. Future profit projections are then discounted back to their current value. So, let's say an analyst follows a stock that is currently $18 per share and projects its earnings for the current fiscal year to be $1.25 per share. Figuring the stock should sell at an industry-typical P/E ratio of 20, the analyst projects that the stock *should be* around $25 per share, at least when those earnings are realized. A purchase at 18 would therefore yield the potential of a 39-percent gain (minus transaction costs and taxes), once the stock sells at what the analyst says is its intrinsic value. This would naturally represent an above-average return on most measures, assuming that the stock does not entail any unusual risks. In its simplest form, this is the essence of fundamental stock research, and the projected price of 25 is the analyst's estimate of the stock's intrinsic value.

On the surface, it's easy to be swayed by this seemingly attractive situation, particularly when accompanied by the analyst's ten-page report justifying that conclusion and the persuasive arguments of an enthusiastic broker. Indeed, if this were something that was clearly selling at less than market value, you might be able to convert such a deal into a tidy profit in a very short time. In the 1970s, my former landlord, Dr. McCormack, had an elderly widow as a patient who asked if he would help her get rid of her late husband's 1943 Rolls-Royce that was collecting dust in her garage. The widow accepted an offer of $11,000 for the Rolls; with another $2,000 in repairs and cleanup, the good doctor had himself a $30,000 collector's item. In weak moments, we let ourselves actually think we can find undiscovered deals like this in the stock market, but it rarely happens in reality. There are no secret stocks owned by people who don't understand their true value. Determining what a 1943 Rolls might be worth only took a few phone calls. You cannot replicate that for stocks. Unfortunately, we see numerous stocks exhibit gains like that of the Rolls in a matter of just days or weeks, and we are greatly tantalized by this seemingly easy money. Situations like that do occur, but you'll rarely find one as a result of an analyst having discovered it by performing fundamental analysis. And even if the analyst did uncover a stock with unusual potential, you would be among thousands of people reading about it at the same time.

When we pull the curtain aside to reveal the source of an analyst's financial wizardry, we find the concept of determining an intrinsic value riddled with complex issues when applied to stocks. It works just fine on instruments like bonds. Knowing current interest rates, a bond's coupon and maturity, and the issuer's credit risk, one can easily value almost any standard bond, and market value will tend to be quite close to what you calculate it should be. Having independent rating agencies (like Moody's and Standard & Poor's) that evaluate the credit risk of bond issuers for you reduces the task to a few clicks on a business calculator. Stocks, however, are a very different story.

Analysts have to stretch the principles of finance to their extremes in order to value stocks. They may start by approaching stocks from the same perspective as bonds—determining the expected payout stream and discounting that back to a current value. But stocks that pay out their entire income as dividends are practically nonexistent, and those that pay out even a portion of their income are in the minority. The analysis is thus complicated by the necessity of building in the internal rate of return to the company, since it is reinvesting net income rather than paying it to shareholders. Then there is the issue of projecting a stock's net income stream in the first place. There is, of course, no fixed maturity to a stock, so the income stream is indefinite. Financial models don't like indefinite. For another thing, income streams for companies are irregular, to say the least, and can sometimes even be negative. Determining an income stream to any level of accuracy at all is done for perhaps one to three years forward at most. Beyond that, everyone acknowledges that it would be somewhere between a gross approximation and a total guess. Once an income projection is made, an analyst uses his or her own judgment to assign a multiple to those earnings that is deemed to be "appropriate" for the stock, given the average multiples on earnings of similar stocks. This requires a hefty amount of judgment on the part of the analyst, especially since price multiples are determined by the market rather than by formula, and multiples change all the time. These and other factors tend to render financial valuations for stocks that are about as accurate as the distances between Earth and the stars in distant solar systems.

The single most important element in determining the intrinsic value of most stocks is the estimate of future earnings. These estimates can vary widely, depending on who is performing the analysis. When an analyst projects earnings, it is usually on a macro level—meaning the analyst will take recent earnings numbers and look at the major influences that are deemed to affect that number going forward (like new products, cost trends, general market demand, economic factors, etc.). The analyst cannot possibly know enough to perform a bottom-up analysis of every product line in the company and all of the possible cost issues. Even the best efforts inside a company to accomplish that are rife with challenges.

I served as a senior executive in a number of smaller companies and, even as an insider, I was highly challenged to make projections I was comfortable with for future business revenues just one year out—much less three years or five years. You never have all the information you really need. Even as an insider, information is surprisingly difficult to get, particularly about the future. Projecting product revenues depends on a huge number of factors: economic variables, marketing variables, actions of competitors, acceptance of new products, timing of new products, effectiveness of marketing plans, amount of marketing expenditures, customer attrition, new customers acquired, manufacturing issues, shipping issues, executive or staff turnover, and a host of unforeseen things. If it was difficult internally, just imagine how much more challenging it is for an external analyst.

Other complexities commonly plague fundamental analysis:

- There is no single method of determining an intrinsic value used by all analysts for all companies. Companies are way too dissimilar to value by any single methodology. There are at least a half-dozen commonly used methodologies. Some are more appropriate for mature companies with strong and steady earnings flows. Others are better-suited to companies with erratic earnings but substantial and valuable fixed assets. Others are geared to companies in high-growth mode that have no earnings at all. Valuation methods can easily vary over time for the same company, and the results of multiple methods are frequently averaged together when a company does not easily fit into a single category.

- Valuations are relative. Earnings multiples are arbitrarily compared to those of other companies in the same industry or with similar business models without necessarily considering that multiples on industry groups vary over time or that the entire industry segment might be under- or overvalued.

- Many companies are diversified into multiple business units, each of which might fit into a different industry segment and that would need to be valued differently. A decent-sized public company might easily have hundreds of different products or thousands of store locations. Analysts can't possibly hope to be on top of all that.

- Analysts frequently have to make personal judgments on the economic effects of management changes, new technologies, and new business models for the companies they analyze.

The factors that go into a calculation of a stock's intrinsic value don't generally change minute to minute or even day to day. But stock prices in the market, of course, do. Therefore, fundamental analysis can, at best, only serve as a rough guide for where a stock *should* trade in the market. And as all of us know, it doesn't matter at all that a stock should trade at a certain price—it only matters where it is actually trading when you want or need to sell it. Fundamental analysis is a methodology that is simply incapable of explaining the gyrations in stock prices. Such gyrations are explained away as unpredictable "noise" caused by temporary factors (like ill-informed investors who don't know any better). Fundamental devotees claim that noise factors tend to offset each other and that stocks *eventually* tend to gravitate back to their fair value. "Eventually" has no particular time limit, mind you, and could easily mean many years.

Since price gyrations in the stock market are an undeniable reality, and since many serendipitous events will inevitably occur with regard to stocks, analysts have to justify their research in light of these factors. Accepted financial practice deals with this by acknowledging that unforeseen factors will occur and having us diversify our holdings to the point at which our portfolios will *statistically* experience as many positive surprises as negative ones. That effectively cancels the net effects of these surprises, leaving us with a high confidence of achieving the average long-term expected return from stocks. There are formulas that suggest how much to diversify and how much volatility (i.e., surprise) to expect if you don't. Once we heed the conventional wisdom and diversify our holdings, we can then pretty much expect to achieve a long-term return in line with the market, though reduced by the amount of money we pay to manage the account. As such, the fundamental approach is inadequate for anything other than garnering a long-term return commensurate with the major market averages and hoping that we are able to survive long enough for the statistics to work themselves out.

## WHY IS WALL STREET FIXATED ON FUNDAMENTALS?

In case it hasn't dawned on you already, the securities industry's mission is not to make you wealthy any more than the fast-food industry's mission is to help you develop a healthier diet. It is to transact and distribute securities products and to generate fees for financial and investment advice. If you look at where the biggest sources of profit are for the large brokerages, you'll also notice that a big part of their mission is to lend you money in the form of margin so you can buy more securities and to trade for their own account. Their profit motive is not in any way tied to making you wealthy, nor is that the mission of your individual broker. As long as you remain with your brokerage firm, it will make money through transaction fees, sales commissions, markups, margin spreads, or investment management fees. The firm would certainly prefer that you make money to increase the chances of your remaining with it, but maximizing your wealth is not the firm's priority.

For decades, Wall Street's business model to the public was to sell stocks and bonds and earn a commission for doing so. No sale, no commission, no matter how much of their expertise they imparted to you. The people hired as commissioned brokers weren't financial experts who were taught to sell—they were salespeople who were taught enough finance to pass the licensing exam. When I was shopping around for a job in my early days on Wall Street, several firms rejected me for a position as a licensed broker because I had an MBA. They said I would be more likely to succeed as a broker if I had sold cars for those two years.

Wall Street has grown up since then and has begun the long process of reinventing itself as asset managers rather than as commissioned salespeople. But the transition is by no means complete, and the mentality created over decades still persists. That mentality survives on the premise that fundamental research is the only way anyone can know what stocks to buy. Research is not proprietary knowledge that your broker creates and no one else has. In a sense, it is simply a marketing tool.

Another reason brokers stand behind fundamental research is that it has the general support of the public, the regulatory bodies, the academic community, and the legal community. That support is paramount when trying to come up with recommendations to fit hundreds of thousands of clients. Wall Street needs a method that can be utilized to manage its entire client base—one that is consistent and can be uniformly implemented. There are two primary business models in the securities industry: transaction-oriented business, where the broker gets paid a commission only when you buy or sell something; and ongoing asset management, where you pay a fee to have your portfolio managed professionally. Fundamental research supports the two business models very well. The transaction-oriented broker uses it to solicit a transaction from you to buy or sell stocks. The asset manager uses it to accumulate stocks and build portfolios on your behalf.

Because the fundamental approach is sanctioned by the right support organizations, it is the safe road to take. As long as a firm uses that approach, it can make recommendations inside a shield of public acceptance, regardless of how right, wrong, or mediocre those recommendations turn out to be. It is extremely important in the investment world to maintain a consistent approach to stock evaluation and a consistent message to the public. By using the "accepted" methodologies for analyzing stocks, brokerage and money-management firms play it safe.

Another important reason has been shared with me by portfolio managers. For anyone or any firm that manages money, the risk of being wrong far outweighs the need to be different. Because investment management itself has become such a commodity service, there is tremendous pressure to perform with consistency. While outperformance is nice, it is not necessary to be successful. What is necessary is holding on to your client base. As long as you consistently perform near the benchmark averages, you will generally keep your clients, even if they are losing money. In other words, there are huge incentives to maintain consistent performance even if mediocre, as long as it is close to the averages, while there is little incentive, coupled with a great deal of risk, to going out on a limb in an attempt to achieve notably better performance than the averages. As such, there is little reason for either a portfolio manager or an investment firm to go outside the accepted guidelines of investment analysis and management. Hedge funds are an exception to this as most are specifically created to take a different road than conventional public funds. They are, however, only available by law to high-net worth clients and institutions, and there are significant questions currently being raised as to whether they perform sufficiently better than conventional funds, given their substantially higher management fees.

The pros in the investment management game know that, at best, their process is guaranteed to produce returns commensurate with the market averages, and that over time those returns will be somewhat mediocre. They know there will be down years and flat years, but they weather those periods together as a group, knowing that other brokers and portfolio managers will suffer commensurately, and that they will likely retain most of their clients because it was the "market's fault" and not theirs. Differences in how the market values a stock from how an analyst values it are considered the market's fault as well. The market must be ignorant of the facts. I cannot think of a single other occupation (except perhaps politics) where the professionals are accorded such wide latitude for error.

Analysts and their firms steadfastly defend their technique (after all, it is their livelihood and a heck of a good one at that) by repeating a mantra of sales slogans so often that they actually grow to believe them. These include the ones that say long-term equity investing has always proven worthwhile and that those who ride through the downtrend are eventually rewarded for their patience. Of course they will always be able to produce some kind of performance statistic that is designed to give you the impression that they consistently match or beat the S&P or some other benchmark comparison, which can't be true, of course, for every money manager out there. Meanwhile, your after-fee, after-tax return stinks, while the market gyrates wildly, giving or taking away an entire year's return objective in a week and doing that repeatedly during the course of the year.

So a legion of sell-side analysts (those at brokerage firms) and buy-side analysts (those at institutional investment organizations) continue to perform fundamental research every day in accordance with the teachings of finance instructors at the major universities and industry schools, and they practice it to the exclusion of almost any other approach. The basic premise underneath this ubiquitous activity is that it is the only acceptable way to value stocks and manage stock portfolios, as ineffective as it has been proven to be. This practice is so embedded into today's thinking that laws governing how trillions of dollars in mutual funds, retirement plans, and trust accounts are invested acknowledge this as the sanctioned and "prudent" way of managing money.

But the bottom line for fundamental financial analysis is that while essential as a starting point, it does not explain stock behavior and can only be relied on to generate overall market returns commensurate with the long-term averages. Once stocks openly trade in the secondary market, something else happens. Other factors clearly come into play. Wall Street knows this but refuses to address nonfinancial variables. Instead, it has dug in its heels to defend its age-old technique as the only answer and to declare the "other factors" as mere undecipherable noise. I think most of us intuitively know what those other factors are.

## WHAT'S ABSENT FROM FUNDAMENTAL ANALYSIS?

There is nothing inherently "wrong" about fundamental analysis, unless, of course, false assumptions are made or bad data utilized. From a financial perspective, fundamental analysis is about as comprehensive a process as you can get. And since fundamental factors are rarely measured more often than monthly or quarterly, it would be almost impossible for a finance geek to wake up one morning and uncover some overlooked fundamental variable or find an obscure relationship between price and other financial variables that explains the variation in stock prices day to day. There simply has to be other factors—nonfinancial ones—that affect stock prices in the open market. This doesn't come as a surprise. They have been right in front of us for a very long time, though they are difficult to measure and to quantify. They are common in all kinds of other markets and have been talked about and alluded to for decades with regard to stocks.

The factors that are absent in fundamental stock analysis are the human factors. Not the employees who work for the company issuing stock: the humans who buy and sell the stock, humans like you, me, Uncle Harry, Martha Stewart, traders, brokers, portfolio managers, money managers, mutual fund and hedge fund managers, and millions of others. Why should stocks be any different than anything else we buy or sell? We may incorporate financial-based logic in our decisions to buy and sell stocks, but it's senseless to deny that our emotions and biases don't have an impact as well. The stock market has some unique characteristics, to be sure, but it's a market nonetheless, and market consists of people buying and selling to each other. So why shouldn't stocks be subjected to the behavioral and psychological characteristics of the people who actively participate in that market—whether in a professional role or acting for themselves? Once a company sells its stock to the public through an IPO, prices float up or down with supply and demand. Once supply and demand are involved, the human factor inevitably enters the market and the underlying fundamentals of the company become little more than a vague reference point in the determination of the stock price.

With this in mind, we can now look at a number of important reasons why stock prices tend to vacillate as much as they do (when we know that fundamentals are not changing that rapidly):

1. **The vagaries of intrinsic value.** There is inherent difficulty in determining even an approximate intrinsic value as a reference point. As discussed earlier in this chapter, intrinsic value at any point in time is not an absolute. If anything, it is more likely a range of prices (and many analysts will actually describe it that way). If the majority of investors believe that XYZ is worth between 35 and 40, then it is logical to assume the stock will continually vary within this range to accommodate supply and demand.

2. **Speculation.** Because it is so easy to trade stocks and the markets are so liquid, stocks are the vehicle of choice for speculators, whether individual or professional. By speculation, I refer to buying strictly for the purpose of selling for a profit in a fairly short time horizon. It would be naïve to assume that speculation (synonymous to many with the term *trading*) does not exacerbate price swings. When the real estate market was hot in 2004–2005, people who might never otherwise speculate on real estate came out of the woodwork to buy second and third homes strictly with the idea of flipping them for a profit in the not-too-distant future. Their view of price was completely set by their expectation of future profits rather than by any more salient method. This happens every day with individual stocks. Huge numbers of people specifically look to buy stocks that are "breaking out" or running up on elevated volume. Similarly, lots of people wait for sell-offs so they can pick up stocks at a bargain for a quick trade. In other words, there are so many people with so many

different approaches to stock trading that it's no surprise stocks move all over the place, even while their fundamentals remain essentially unchanged.

3. **Anticipation.** Everyone knows that to make quick money in stocks, you cannot just react to news, you must anticipate it. Anticipation has become endemic to stock trading, and it is frequently based on hunch more than anything else. The suspicion that one might be wrong is all that is needed to undo a trade, and this surely affects volatility.

4. **Head games.** Market participants are constantly trying to outguess other participants about where stocks are going. This creates a huge variety of cross-currents that I will simply refer to right now as *head games*. Participants are influenced (spooked) very easily by market activity itself, in addition to news and rumors. There is an almost constant sense that other market players know more than you—traders, exchange specialists, institutions, and corporate insiders. Their actions send a variety of cues and miscues to others. As an example, a product like a car, with a lower-than-usual price, will generally bring buyers rushing in to scoop up the bargain quickly. But with stocks, a lower price can also be interpreted as a danger signal. It may mean that others are dumping and may know something you don't. Thus, some buyers may actually view a lower price as a negative rather than a positive. This makes the market for stocks rather unique and even more subject to volatility. (Later, this will be described as *behavioral factors* and explained in much more detail in Chapter 7.)

5. **News reports.** The media has its own special way of contributing to market mayhem. Here's a typical example. All three of these headlines appeared in the *Wall Street Journal* on April 16, 2008:

Earnings Slump at J.P. Morgan,
And Continued Stress Is Expected

Wells Fargo's Net Declines 11%
As Credit-Loss Provision Surges

> Stocks rallied after better-than-expected quarterly results from J.P. Morgan and Wells Fargo boosted sentiment.

All three were true, but you had to read through the articles to discover why the apparent anomaly existed. News is so widely anticipated nowadays that when it finally hits the press, it is frequently not just anticlimactic, but counterintuitive. The losses above were definitely bad news for the two institutions mentioned, but they had been so widely anticipated, and presumably built into the stock prices already, that when the details were actually released and slightly less onerous than had been expected, the news was taken as a big plus and the stocks rallied sharply. The old adage on Wall Street "Buy on the rumor and sell on the news" has more truth these days than ever.

6. **Market sentiment.** Most people will acknowledge that the stock market itself fluctuates with investor mood or sentiment. We can easily observe that on days when there is overriding news on the economy, natural disasters, or geopolitical conflicts, the sentiment on the entire stock market rises or lessens accordingly and is influenced by factors other than the specific company or industry financials of individual stocks. Like a rising and lowering tide, it takes most stocks with it on these moves. There is good reason to believe that this overall effect is always there and simply more obvious on certain days. (Much more on this in Chapter 7.)

Except for the first, all of these reasons are nonfinancial and related to the way market participants perceive and react to stocks rather than to material changes in the fundamentals of those stocks. A substantial amount of opinion from stock strategists and financial luminaries throughout the last century points to human behavior and psychology, for better or worse, as the primary factor that renders fundamental analysis ineffective at pegging stock prices. Today, the trendy term for the study of the human factor in stock pricing is *behavioral finance*, and there's a growing body of research that supports it.

## CHAPTER NOTES

1. "Benjamin Graham: The Father of Security Analysis," Available online at http://www.afterquotes.com/great/people/ben-graham/index.htm.
2. *Wall Street Journal* online, Company Research, Analysts Ratings, September 12, 2008 (sourced from First Call/Thompson Financial).
3. Benjamin Mark Cole, *The Pied Pipers of Wall Street* (New York: Bloomberg Press, 2001), p. xiii.
4. Securities and Exchange Commission. Press release, April 28, 2003.
5. Benjamin Graham and David L. Dodd, *Security Analysis*, 1940 edition, p. 16.

# Subjective Value    **3**

---

*People are largely concerned, not with making superior long term forecasts of the profitable yield on an investment over its whole life, but with foreseeing changes in the conventional basis of valuation a short time ahead of the general public.*

JOHN MAYNARD KEYNES

I F FUNDAMENTAL ANALYSIS by itself is unable to provide valuations for stocks that explain the changing prices determined by the market, then we need to adopt a different method of price valuation, one that incorporates significant value from behavioral influences. This chapter opens a door to an approach to stock valuation that combines fundamental economic analysis with a subjective component to account for behavioral factors.

Marketing and advertising people spend untold amounts of time and money specifically trying to formulate an impression in our minds about companies and their products. They exploit even the subtlest differences to distinguish themselves from competitors. They use slogans, images, celebrities, and even specific colors to create impressions that will steer consumers subconsciously toward their products. To think that we as investors can set all that aside and focus purely on financials when we buy stocks is to ignore a basic and oft-proven fact about human behavior: that we are influenced by such advertising more than we might want to believe, and we cannot turn those impressions off like a switch.

That doesn't mean we don't consider the financial or investment opportunity in stocks we buy—it just means that other factors, some we are not even consciously aware of, are also present. Ask people why they buy the stocks they do and you'll get a wide array of answers. Most individual investors probably can't even tell you what the projected earnings or the price multiples are for the stocks they buy. Brokers have known for decades that people buy stocks on impressions and on the all-important "story," and anyone who has ever been pitched by a broker has heard one or more of the following: "The company is a prime takeover candidate." "The insiders have been buying thousands of shares." "Their next [movie, drug, chip] is really going to be a big winner." "The only reason the stock is down is because the market is soft." "They have some gangbuster new products coming out." "They've signed some big new contracts, and their earnings are about to explode." "They are set to do business in China." The list goes on and on. There are usually some numbers to back this up, but the numbers are the "steak" and the story is the "sizzle," as they say. Beyond the sizzle are impressions that lie in the recesses of our minds that come to bear when buying shares of a company we're familiar with.

As a broker, I encountered this all the time. One particular investment we sold at E. F. Hutton in the early 1980s was a limited partnership called Silver Screen Partners. It was a partnership to make five movies with Walt Disney Company. Investors put up the money, Disney made the movies, and the returns were shared even though the investors were given a modest fixed return of around 7 percent and participated only slightly in any big upside. If you read the fine print, you'd know that even if the movie was a blockbuster, Disney and the key movie personnel were going to get most, if not all, of that upside. Disney did make some guarantees that investors would be made whole if the movies weren't made or if they bombed. In other words, it wasn't going to ever be a big winner, and the return was likely to be something less than the 7 percent overall unless all five movies were winners. At that time, a bond with such characteristics would normally have been met with a yawn, but Silver Screen Partners was a sellout. As it turns out, the movies were made and did reasonably well. The partnership paid back sums of the invested capital as the movies were released and then small dividends for years as the movies were circulated. The investors did okay but never made big money despite the fact that several of the movies actually did very well. Despite the risks of moviemaking and the uncertainty of returns, the partnership sold like hotcakes. Why? The Disney allure and the opportunity to own a piece of a movie.

The power and influence of an investment "story" is not confined to small, uneducated investors by any means. The epitome of buying on emotion and not on concrete analysis was brought to light by the Bernard Madoff affair. Thousands of presumably savvy individuals and a host of money managers, banks, and other professionals invested billions of dollars with Madoff based entirely on the sizzle of steady double-digit annual returns and the appeal of dealing with an industry icon. The secret sauce of his supposed methodology and his aura as an exclusive hard-to-get manager only added to the mystique. His investment methodology was not only flawed but also totally fictitious! Without even looking at a single client statement, any of the students in my options class at Berkeley would be able to shoot holes in Madoff's claimed split-strike conversion methodology. The ability of so many supposedly intelligent people (professionals who are licensed and paid to manage money, no less) getting sucked into a scam of that magnitude speaks volumes about the reliance on emotion that exists in the investment community.

Because of their money-earning nature, businesses and their stocks are predominantly valued by industry gurus from an economic perspective. That means determining the economic benefit (i.e., net income) to be expected, weighing the risk or uncertainty of that income benefit, and determining what that justifies in present-day price. For better or worse, however, that is not necessarily the way the investing public—or even many investment professionals— think about stocks. We tend to simplify the decision process down to a few key items, and the calculations are reduced to what we can easily do in our heads. So, while an economic valuation is certainly justified in part, it is not justified as the sole price determinant from the perspective of market participants. Therein lies the essence of the problem with fundamental analysis. It does not consider the human or subjective factors that make their way into stock prices.

## A MORE SUBJECTIVE APPROACH TO VALUATION

There is a subjective component to stock pricing, just like there is with almost anything else people buy. Investors build it into their market assessments, and analysts build it into their valuations. By nature, it is highly variable and differs from person to person and among stocks. It can grow to egregious extremes—as was the case with Internet and biotech stocks—or it can even be negative, as occurs when the public prices a stock below its economic value and the company either repurchases its own shares or some other company comes in and buys the company out. Bear in mind that the economic value itself is not an absolute and that all parties will not agree on exactly what it is at any given time.

Applying common rules, we could conceivably determine a base economic value for any business. Inherent to those rules would be an application of standardized current value techniques that minimize the subjectivity added to valuations by analysts. We would then define the amount by which the company's market price exceeds this base economic value as the subjective component. In essence, the economic value would be akin to the intrinsic value that analysts currently calculate but without the inflated earnings multiples that analysts presume on behalf of the market. In this manner, the base economic value of a public company would be reduced to something more akin to the values typically assigned to small or private companies (discussed further later). Under these guidelines, it's likely that the subjective component would actually be greater than the base economic value for most companies.

Subjective factors are likely adding a substantial premium to the fundamental value of individual stocks, despite the opposing classical view that the market prices publicly traded companies more efficiently (i.e., closer to intrinsic value) because of liquidity. This premium, embedded into the prices of all publicly traded stocks, includes subjective factors such as the following:

- going concern premium,
- convenience premium,
- popularity premium, and
- anticipation premium.

### Going Concern Premium

Part of the premium we pay in stock price traces back to the value created during the formation of the company. At every company's inception, a substantial investment is made (both in time and money) in transforming a bunch of assets into a functioning, self-sustaining business. The initial investors take on that risk knowing that they will lose everything invested if the company does not succeed but will realize a substantial "going concern premium" if the company has been successful when they sell their shares. This is the underlying premise behind seed and venture capital, and the way these investors capitalize on it most effectively is when the company goes public because the public can always be counted on to pay the going concern premium. This premium remains (and likely grows) in the value of the company, as all businesses logically carry a value greater than the sum of their net assets just for being a going concern . . . until, of course, they cease to be one.

When we buy shares on the secondary market, we pay that premium because it is incorporated into the price, and we do so with the idea that the stock will continue to carry it when we sell it. We view that as the multiple of expected earnings for the stock; in our minds, we tend to consider it in light of the probability of next year's (or even next quarter's) earnings meeting expectations without even considering the possibility that the company may potentially disappear altogether. Analysts are not immune to such thinking—when was the last time you saw one even suggest the remote possibility that a company might not exist in the future? (Except, perhaps, once the stock is trading for pennies per share and bankruptcy is imminent.) By ignoring the possibility, no matter how remote, that the stock we're buying might actually cease to exist, we bear an additional risk. That risk may be extremely small under normal year-to-year business conditions, but to holders of Enron, WorldCom, Bear Stearns, General Motors, Merrill Lynch, Chrysler, and a slew of others, that risk is a long way from nil. Shareholders who buy on the secondary market bear not only the normal risk of earnings shortfalls but also the risk of losing the going concern premium built up and carried in the stock's price.

We tend to think that once a company is well established, bankruptcy and liquidation are so remote as to be unworthy of consideration, but that risk comes back to haunt us in tough times. Even classic stock-valuation models such as the capital asset pricing model (CAPM) account only for a stock's risk as measured by its beta—its tendency to *continually* move up or down with the general market. It does not account for the potential *discontinuity* of its demise. While an admittedly low overall probability of occurrence across the full range of public companies in any given year, the consequence of that occurrence is catastrophic. People have built entire neighborhoods in the lava path of Mount Ranier, a volcano that scientists deem to still be active. The perception must evidently be that the chances of the mountain erupting during any one person's lifetime are virtually nonexistent, but that is not so. The chance may be remote, but it will clearly be catastrophic if it does happen. We tend not to follow logical rules for estimation, particularly where probability of occurrence is small but magnitude of occurrence is large. As Nassim Nicholas Taleb comments in *Fooled by Randomness*, "It does not matter how frequently something succeeds if failure is too costly to bear."[1]

### CONVENIENCE PREMIUM

There is another premium built into the shares we buy on the secondary market—a premium similar to the one we pay for milk at 7-Eleven versus milk at Safeway. We pseudo-investors pay a healthy premium for the convenience of being able to buy or sell the stock of any one of thousands of public companies with a phone call or a few mouse clicks. A recent study published in the *Journal of Finance* concluded that, "Capital market transactions essentially bundle a primary transaction for the underlying security with a secondary transaction for immediacy. From this perspective, the price of immediacy explains the wedge between transaction prices and fundamental value, and therefore represents a cost of transacting."[2] This immediacy premium is represented in magnitude by the relative size of bid–ask spreads in addition to the premium (or discount) exacted by specialists and market makers for facilitating large transactions. As a transactional cost, it would be expected to hinder overall performance over time, and it acts as additional risk when viewed as the cost of entry and exit for large positions.

## POPULARITY PREMIUM: THE "WINNER'S CURSE"

The U.S. stock market may suffer from its own popularity, and we as participants consequently suffer the winner's curse. We have placed the stock market on a pedestal and have made it the investment of choice in this country. Among worldwide populations, Americans are notoriously poor savers but aggressive investors. The ease of buying and selling stocks coupled with the presumed safety and attractive growth prospects of U.S. corporations drive us to the equity markets like lemmings to the sea. We are hopelessly addicted to equities, despite periodic crashes that become quickly recast as long-term bargains. Millions of people fund their own retirement plans through individual retirement accounts, 401(k)s, and other qualified retirement plans, many of which funnel money directly from paychecks into the stock market via mutual funds.

As a result, there is simply too much money chasing too few stocks. The amount of money flowing into the market is often way more than the amount needed to absorb the new stock being added to the market. This has become further exacerbated by huge flows of foreign money into our stock market—not just by sovereign wealth funds and institutions but also by individuals the world over who can watch our markets and trade as easily as we can on the Internet.

It is almost impossible to determine how much net new money actually flows into U.S. stocks each year, but it may be driving our market to persistent overvaluation, which both investors and analysts have come to take for granted. When demand exceeds supply for bonds, it is evident in their market price or in the drop in net yields. As money flowed out of the stock market into U.S. Treasury securities in late 2008, we saw the yields on those securities go to zero and even dip into the negative as prices rose because of demand. It is more difficult to identify when stocks are overvalued because stock valuations are imprecise and vary considerably over time, making it almost impossible to define exactly what constitutes overvaluation in the first place.

Nonetheless, it is at least evident that over the last century, price-to-earnings (P/E) multiples on the Standard & Poor's (S&P) 500 Index have been rising and that in the last thirty years or so that rise has accelerated.

**FIGURE 3.1** shows P/E multiples for the S&P 500 between 1881 and 2008 as compiled by Robert J. Shiller. Examining the multiples for the 100 years between 1881 and 1980, we get an average P/E of 14.83. Over the 28 years from 1981 to 2008, however, the average P/E expanded to 21.74, thanks in part to the Internet bubble of the late 1990s. While this does not constitute proof of overvaluation, it certainly indicates that valuations have been significantly (i.e., 50 percent) higher on average than during the preceding 100 years.

With so many people around the world fixated on the U.S. stock market and such an enormous amount of money automatically flowing in through retirement funds and other major sources on a regular basis, it is easy to see how this overvaluation would be the result. One cannot dismiss this idea by saying that market forces are efficient and will tend to bring prices down to reality. Prices do correct periodically, but under normal conditions that may actually represent the popularity premium simply getting larger and smaller.

As a result, we suffer from a phenomenon called the *winner's curse*. Behavioral finance author Richard H. Thaler penned a book about

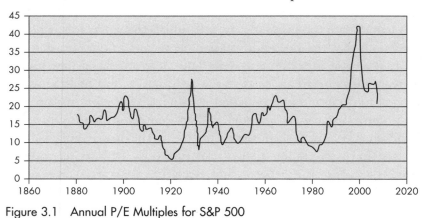

Figure 3.1   Annual P/E Multiples for S&P 500

Source: Robert J. Shiller, compiled for *Irrational Exuberance* (Princeton, NJ: Princeton University Press, 2005).

the paradoxes and anomalies of economic life, titling it with that very name. The winner's curse is a paradox about losing as one is winning. It is exemplified by Thaler in a scenario in which a speculator is interested in bidding for land to be used for oil exploration. As he learns that more bidders will be involved, his instinct is to raise the bid price in order to increase the chances of winning. However, if he is not careful, he can end up winning the auction, while paying more for the land than can be drawn from it and thereby also losing. We suffer this curse periodically in the stock market, buying more and more stock until the market has become overvalued and subjects us all to a healthy correction. We lose by winning, and we keep doing it over and over again.

### ANTICIPATION PREMIUM

The psychology behind stock purchases is a complex game of anticipation. Whatever degree of market efficiency you ascribe to, most people (and numerous academic studies) acknowledge that one cannot be a successful investor by sitting back, reading news, and making investment decisions on that basis. You must anticipate . . . and to be successful, you must anticipate correctly both in timing and magnitude often enough to make up for the times you will be wrong. The market is rife with anticipation. And since the vast majority of positions are long, that anticipation manifests itself into purchase behavior and premium pricing.

We are also taught that the market has a continuous upward bias, and therefore the natural behavior is to purchase now rather than later. Why wait and risk paying more? The confidence that the market is always going to go up from where it is now and the fear that we may lose out on potential gains by waiting has been continually thrust on investors by the brokerage industry. This, too, contributes to a persistent tendency toward overvaluation.

We know these valuation premiums exist, but we tend to accept them under the assumption that they are always there, so they will be priced into the securities when we sell. That is a naïve assumption. These premiums vary because they are largely subjective, and any component of price that is subjective is going to be influenced more by human behavior than by fundamentals.

## A LIFE-CYCLE VIEW OF SUBJECTIVE VALUE

Subjective value is affected by many variables. For one thing, it varies with all businesses over the life of the business. When a business is in its infancy, initial capital is invested at high risk due to the lack of net earnings and the uncertainty of success. Until the company generates earnings and demonstrates viability, its value from both an economic and subjective standpoint is extremely low. In the event the business doesn't succeed, some assets may be able to be sold, but the economic value will be close to zero if the company folds in most cases. The subjective component of the business value is very high given that initial investors know there is no immediate economic value but invest anyway. If you invest in a start-up that is not yet profitable, you know that it is high risk and that the share of the company you are buying will likely have little or no value if the company goes bust. Therefore, such investments ascribe a value to those shares that is almost entirely subjective. Once a business crosses over into profitability or at least generates positive earnings, its value increases dramatically because it now can be sold as a going business and thus picks up economic value. A large part of the value is still determined subjectively during the early years, but the subjective component becomes a less significant portion of the total value.

Adolescence is the period of high growth a company enjoys in its early years. It now has both economic value and subjective value. The subjective value centers on the impression investors have of the company's ultimate potential, and this value will likely be greater for companies with big potential upside than for companies in more steady or predictable businesses. Once a company goes public, the value of its shares is determined by the price of the stock, with the market now deciding the subjective value. In theory, as earnings increase and the business matures, the economic factors grow and take on more of a role in the valuation. The subjective component thus starts to decrease. Meanwhile, though, as business cycles come and go and various factors affect the fundamentals of the company, its economic value may wax and wane, or at least have periods of more accelerated growth and periods of lesser growth. So, too, does the subjective value wax and wane with the company's outlook and other factors.

At maturity, the value of a company shifts even more toward its economic component again as growth slows and subjective value peaks. Once uncertainty is reduced, and the company becomes a cash cow, the value of the company drops toward its economic component. There can still be a good amount of subjective value, but the economic value becomes increasingly prominent.

When liquidation becomes imminent, the value of a business reverts to economic or simply asset value, depending on whether it will continue to function in some way. Subjective value is about future potential, which a failing business does not possess. If the business is sold to another company, there is some subjective value in the form of the premium a suitor may need to pay to get shareholders to relinquish their shares. If the company is going out of business, however, then it is strictly worth liquidation or asset value, and that is entirely devoid of any subjective value.

FIGURE 3.2 shows this effect. The idea behind this illustration is not to imply an exact amount of subjective value to a company at any stage but to appreciate how it changes over the life cycle of the business. The economic value changes with fundamentals, but the subjective value changes as the market continually reappraises it. This provides a way of thinking about stocks in more than just fundamental terms.

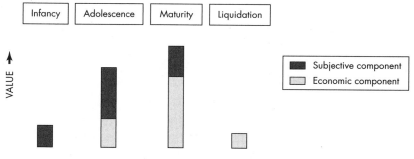

Figure 3.2   Subjective Value over the Business Life Cycle

Subjective value also clearly varies by industry and type of company. Companies in what are perceived to be vibrant, high-growth, high-profile industries will have much more subjective value than those in quiet, dull, or less trendy businesses. And trends vary quite a bit over time. Internet stocks had their day in the late 1990s, biotech companies had theirs in the early 2000s, and energy companies ruled the roost from 2003 through 2008.

## QUANTIFYING SUBJECTIVE VALUE

Traditional finance theory interprets any subjective component of stock value to be a temporary phenomenon, a market anomaly. Traditionalists believe subjective value exists only until the market "gets smart" and recognizes a stock's true value. If the subjective component were small in relation to the stock price, then that might be an acceptable way to look at it. But the subjective value of stocks can be shown to be neither temporary nor insignificantly small.

For a little perspective, let's first look at privately held businesses. It is generally acknowledged that private companies sell for less than their public counterparts (as a multiple of their earnings) due to their relative illiquidity, among other factors. A Willamette Management Associates study on the difference in valuation multiples for private transactions versus public transactions covering hundreds of transactions over nineteen years (of the same companies) measured the discounts on earnings multiples for private transactions at between 40 percent and 63 percent over comparable public transactions.[3]

Another way to view this phenomenon is to say that that the valuations of private businesses more accurately reflect the buyer's appraisal of their base economic value and that public companies are accorded a considerable premium. Buyers of private companies tend to be more interested in the business as a long-term investment, and they would be less inclined to buy for the kind of short-term speculation that a public shareholder would be due to the illiquidity. They are also much more likely to be informed buyers who have conducted at least some due diligence on the target business. For them, it boils down to almost pure economics.

On the other hand, nonparticipating shareholders in public companies tend to distance themselves from the businesses in which they invest. Through mutual funds, pension funds, and other intermediaries, they become, as Keynes suggested in the opening quote of this chapter, even more insulated from the raw economics of the investment and are thus driven more by subjective matters.

Taking the reciprocal of the discounts mentioned above, we would see that public business transactions sold at prices that were between 1.6 and 2.5 times higher than private transactions. The reasons for this may be debatable, but the fact remains that publicly traded companies may sell for double what similar private companies would sell for. And while some of that may be due to economic factors such as cheaper capital and quicker access to it, the market may be adding a considerable subjective component into the mix.

It's distinctly possible that if we were to determine the raw economic value of all public companies, we would find that the majority of the value ascribed to them by the markets is actually subjective. That would go a long way toward explaining why we see so much volatility and why it is not always related to material changes in company fundamentals. Analysts know what the economic value of most companies is. That's where fundamental analysis shines. But analysts then attach a multiple to the earnings to get a more appropriate market value. This "multiple" is little more than a giant fudge factor. There is scant economic justification for multiples. In concept, they should account for the quality of projected earnings and the likelihood those earnings will be realized. But that really isn't the case, and the assignment of a multiple becomes circular when analysts simply benchmark it to the multiples the market has assigned to other companies in similar industry groups. In addition, multiples for industry groups are quite different at different times, yet analysts rarely make an allowance for that when assigning one to their estimates.

Even for the market as a whole, multiples have varied considerably over time. The S&P 500 was selling at a multiple as low as 5 in 1919, frothing up to 32 in 1929, and returning to 5 by 1932. It then reached a spike of 44 in 1999 and was still 32.8 when the market peaked in March 2000. That dropped to 25.7 by October 2002 and was around 18 by September 2007.[4]

Of course, there are valid economic reasons why multiples would expand and contract, like interest rates and business cycles, but not to the degree noted above. The reality is that the market is willing to pay a whole heck of a lot more per unit of earnings at some times than others, and much of this variation may be ascribed to subjective influences.

Judging by what happens when multiples get too high, we can see that the subjective part of a stock's value accounts for much of the risk in the stock. The subjective part also frequently accounts for the upside potential. The subjective part encompasses how trendy the stock or its industry is and how much cachet it has. Every industry has its favorites—companies that are priced in the market at a higher multiple of earnings than others in the same industry. Most of the reasons for this are subjective. People like management. People like the company's image. They like its advertising. In short, the subjective value of a stock is the premium (or discount) over its economic value that people are willing to pay. It's no different than why you are willing to pay more for that silver Lexus than the black one.

As noted above, private business transactions gave us a clue as to just how much of a stock price might be subjectively determined. Basic finance actually provides another way to do it (and comes up with an answer of similar magnitude). A college-level course in finance will tell you that financial risk and return are statistically related, and that the reason why anyone would assume the risks of owning stocks (or any investment with risk) is the expectation of being accordingly rewarded with a greater return over the long term than the so-called risk-free benchmark as represented by U.S. Treasury bonds. This additional reward for taking the risk in stocks is called the *risk premium*, and you would need to hold your stock portfolio over the long term to realize this reward. *Long term* is typically considered to be at least a year but could easily be five, ten, or even twenty years.

You would also learn that the risks of owning stock are categorized into two types: (1) company-specific or diversifiable risks and

(2) market risks. Company-specific risks include all those particular to an individual stock such as a disappointing new product, a lawsuit for patent infringement, a union strike, or any one of a thousand other reasons why a particular company might not make its numbers and thus fail to provide the expected return to shareholders. They are called *diversifiable* risks because it has been proven that you can eliminate them, statistically at least, by diversifying your holdings with a sufficient number of stocks that are relatively different from one another (i.e., different industries). That way, the odds are that for every stock in the portfolio that does unexpectedly worse than expected, another will be as likely to do better than expected. A portfolio of sixty to 100 stocks does a very nice job of fulfilling this statistical requirement, but even twenty or so stocks gets one most of the way toward eliminating the company-specific risks inherent in any one stock, at least statistically.

Academic finance also tells us something we have certainly all experienced: the broad universe of stocks suffers a different set of risks than those associated with specific companies. These include the overall state of the economy, geopolitical uncertainties, natural disasters, and that ever convenient catchall called *investor sentiment*, not to mention the thousands of other things that can cause the overall market to go up or down at any time. These are appropriately called *market risks*.

Therefore, investing in a broad enough basket of stocks will immunize your portfolio (at least to some statistical degree) from the unpredictable nature of individual stocks and consequently end up allowing you to achieve a return commensurate with that of the overall market. You cannot, however, immunize yourself from market risks. You simply have to remain in the market long enough to experience the opportunities along with the risks. The overall U.S. stock market as measured by the S&P 500 has a long term (fifty-year plus) upward bias of around 10 percent to 12 percent per year.[5] But even a period as long as eight years might yield zero net return if those eight years were 2000 to 2008.

By looking at the historical movement in any stock, we can calculate an expected return based on the long-term trend of the stock's price, ignoring the warning that the industry is so fond of repeating: "past performance does not guarantee future results." (Bear in mind that what a statistician says we may "expect" is not necessarily how our nonscientific brains define the word.) We can then calculate how far the stock historically varies in price from day to day and call that *volatility*. We allow ourselves to use the volatility as a proxy for the risk in a stock under the premise that markets are efficient and that the market prices each stock above or below its expected value over time, thereby giving us license to assume that future prices will do likewise.

We can now attach some numbers. Volatility is represented as a percentage, and while the volatilities of different stocks can vary from 5 percent to more than 100 percent, an average volatility among diversified stocks is considered to be about 35 percent. The volatility of a large portfolio (such as the S&P 500) is figured to be around 20 percent. (Volatility in a portfolio is always less than that of the individual stocks that compose it, because some will expectedly be going up while others go down.) So, by diversifying into a portfolio, we can reduce the volatility of individual stocks averaging 35 percent to a single volatility of 20 percent for the entire portfolio. By creating a portfolio, we have thus reduced the risk of an average stock by 43 percent. That's all well and good, but it still leaves the portfolio with 20 percent volatility. That is the market risk—the component of stock risk you cannot eliminate.

The impact of this conclusion is that more than half the risk (and accordingly half the expected return) of owning stocks comes from the overall market. Yet virtually all investment analysis is aimed at individual stocks because traditional finance tells us there is no consistent way to assess the risks (or opportunities) in the overall market. Might that be because more than half the value of stocks is subjective?

## CHAPTER NOTES

1. Nassim Nicholas Taleb, *Fooled by Randomness* (New York: Random House, 2004), p. 4.
2. George C. Chacko, "The Price of Immediacy," *Journal of Finance*, 63(3) (June 2008): pp. 1253–1290.

3. Shannon Pratt, Robert Reilly, and Robert Schweihs, *Valuing Small Businesses and Professional Practices* (New York: McGraw Hill, 1998), p. 461.
4. Robert J. Shiller, "Stock Market Data Used in *Irrational Exuberance*—Updated." Available online at www.irrationalexuberance.com/shiller_downloads/ie_data.xls.
5. Allen Shawn, "What Long-Term Return Should We Expect on Large-Capitalization Stock Market Indexes?" (July 2003 and updated February 14, 2006). Available online at www.investorsfriend.com.

# Random and Efficient Markets

**4**

*It is unlikely that the random walk hypothesis provides an exact description of the behavior of stock market prices.*[1]

EUGENE FAMA

WITH ITS ROOTS strongly wrapped around current values of future earnings streams, fundamental analysis performs reasonably well during periods of steady growth and commensurately rising earnings. But at times when earnings are erratic, declining, or affected by significant one-time write-offs, the fundamental method becomes seriously challenged, and the variance between analyst estimates and actual earnings can sometimes render fundamental analysis almost totally unusable. Well into the fall of 2008, and amid the most severe drubbing of stocks in several decades, analysts let their forward-looking earnings estimates get so far behind reality that it was almost laughable. A *Barron's* reporter wrote, "Talk about out of touch: Analysts currently estimate that earnings for the companies in the [Standard & Poor's (S&P) 500 Index] will rise 29 percent in the fourth quarter, and keep climbing, by 15 percent in 2009, to a record $91.41 a share, according to Thomson Reuters. That seems wholly unrealistic, given the recent jump in unemployment, the credit crisis and last week's news that the economy contracted at a 0.3 percent annual pace in the third quarter."[2] The reporter polled a handful of prominent market strategists whose consensus was that earnings for the S&P stocks in 2009 were more likely to come in at around $70, a number far more in keeping with what current market prices are reflecting. By the first quarter of 2009, it was looking like the earnings for the S&P might drop as low as $40 to $50, separating even further from analysts' estimates.

Acknowledging that the determination of a stock's theoretical intrinsic value through classic fundamental analysis is worthless as a short-term investment tool, Wall Street clings to this futile preoccupation on the premise that it has merit in the longer term. Nevertheless, that also remains to be seen. As we know, most fund and portfolio managers fail to beat the market averages over time, and one has to wonder how many fundamentalists are pondering the extension of their definition of "long term" to ten years instead of one, given that market action in the fall of 2008 brings stocks back to where they were in 1998. While Wall Street has been reckoning with this dilemma over the years, academia actually came up with an alternative approach fifty years ago.

## Efficient Market Hypothesis

The alternate view about stocks holds that the stock market itself is an efficient mechanism for pricing stocks at their intrinsic value, and it simply redefines *intrinsic value* as the current price of the stock at any moment in time. This has the practical effect of replacing a theoretical value that cannot be precisely calculated with an actual value, albeit one that changes moment to moment. In this efficient market view, instead of a handful of analysts telling us what they believe the price of a stock should be, tens of thousands of market participants tell us what they think the price should be. Average market participants may not be as educated as professional securities analysts, but they vote with real money. With a healthy dose of both buyers and sellers in the participating audience (and presumably at least some who are financially savvy), this view of stocks implies that the market is an effective means of determining value.

That's the way it has always been in the commodity futures markets. There has never been a concept of intrinsic value for items such as gold or wheat because they do not generate cash flow like companies. Why spend enormous time and money even trying to calculate fair or intrinsic value, much less arguing over whether there is even a way to calculate it at all? What difference does it make that the current price is different from some theoretically determined value? The market price is what it's actually worth if you wanted to buy or sell it, and who knows how long, if ever, the market might take to "correctly" price a security at the calculated intrinsic value? This line of thinking belongs to a view of the stock market called the *efficient market hypothesis* (EMH).

In the 1960s, the efficient market hypothesis began to gain popularity. We could debate at great length whether intrinsic value can be calculated or whether the market price serves as a fair assessment of it, and indeed scholars have for the half century that EMH has been around. But debate is futile and unnecessary unless you're building a dissertation around it. The bottom line is that it doesn't matter. Either way, intrinsic value is a theoretical concept, and stocks fluctuate in a way that traditional finance cannot explain or quantify.

Nevertheless, most of Wall Street and its academic cohorts stand by the notion that traditional principles allow analysts to value a company (and, by implication, its stock) through a detailed evaluation of corporate fundamentals such as earnings projections, capitalization structure, projected cash flows, asset valuations, and a host of other financial factors. This practice is more or less the exclusive method for analyzing stocks and determining (or at least approximating) their intrinsic values. In theory, armed with an intrinsic value, a firm or investment manager could recommend a stock for purchase when its current market price is sufficiently below that or recommend selling the stock if the market price is sufficiently above it. Reality (as most of you already know) is radically different from this scenario.

The factors that go into a calculation of a stock's intrinsic value don't generally change minute to minute or even day to day. But stock prices in the market do, of course. Therefore, fundamental analysis can, at best, only serve as a guide for where a stock *should* trade in the market. And, as all of us know, it doesn't matter at all that a stock should trade at a certain price—it only matters where it is actually trading when you want or need to sell it. Fundamental folks cannot explain the gyrations in stock prices except to say that they incorporate a certain amount of unpredictable "noise" caused by temporary factors (such as ill-informed investors who don't know any better). They claim that such factors tend to offset each other and that stocks *eventually* tend to return to a fair value. "Eventually" has no particular time limit, mind you, and could easily mean many years.

Hardcore fundamentalists can be so intransigent, however, that they feel they are right and the market is wrong. This perversion of pricing logic underscores the entrenchment of the fundamental perspective on investing.

Since there is a significant piece of forecasting involved in fundamental analysis and many serendipitous events are bound to occur, analysts know that they may be surprised or disappointed by actual events as they unfold. They also know from experience that the prices people are willing to transact stocks can vary greatly from intrinsic value—both up and down. Accepted financial practice deals with these inevitabilities by having us diversify our holdings to the point at which our portfolios will statistically experience as many positive surprises as negative ones, thereby offsetting themselves and leaving us with a high confidence of achieving the average long-term expected return from stocks in general. There are formulas that suggest how much to diversify and how much volatility to expect if we don't. Once we heed the conventional wisdom and diversify our holdings, we can then pretty much expect to achieve a long-term return in line with the market, reduced by the amount of money we pay to manage the account. As such, the fundamental approach is inadequate as a portfolio-management tool for anything other than garnering a long-term return commensurate with the major market averages and hoping that we are able to survive long enough for the statistics to work themselves out.

Wall Street (my euphemism for the entire securities industry) has no alternative to fundamental analysis. Unable to deny that there exists variation in market price from intrinsic value, investment managers have deftly manufactured justifications for their continued use of the technique to the exclusion of all others. Those justifications claim that stocks ultimately revert to their intrinsic value and that by buying and holding for the long term, you will eventually see this occur. The problem sometimes is whether your grandchildren might see it occur. Sadly, this concocted, self-justifying line of reasoning is the dominant and almost universal theme among investment managers today.

Portfolio managers almost all work within this analytical framework, tweaking the technique ever so carefully in an attempt to demonstrate returns in close accordance with (or ideally above—though that rarely happens) market averages over time and to do it for a huge mass of people. Such returns over the last fifty years have averaged around 10 percent to 11 percent. Of course, the professionals make their living from management fees, typically around 1 percent or more, so they actually need to beat the long-term averages by a sufficient margin to justify that expense.

Because investment management itself has become such a commodity service, there is tremendous pressure to perform, with consistency being more highly praised than outperformance, at least up to a point. The simple truth in investment management is that there are huge incentives to maintaining consistent performance even if mediocre, as long as it is close to the market averages, and little incentive (coupled with a lot of risk) to going out on a limb in an attempt to achieve notably better performance than the averages. As such, there is little reason for either a manager or an investment firm to go outside the accepted guidelines of investment management. Interestingly, however, hedge funds were designed to do just that, and they have now become hugely popular as a result, though they are only available by law to high-net-worth clients and institutions.

The pros in the investment management game know that, at best, their process is guaranteed to produce returns commensurate with the market averages and that over time those returns can expect to be somewhat mediocre. They know there will be down years and flat years, but they voraciously defend their technique (after all, it *is* their livelihood and a heck of a good one at that) by repeating a mantra of sales slogans so often that they actually believe them now. These include the ones that say long-term equity investing has always proven worthwhile and that those who ride through the down trend are eventually rewarded for their patience. And, of course, they will always be able to produce some kind of performance statistic that is designed to give you the impression that they do, in fact, consistently beat the S&P or some other benchmark comparison—which, of course, can't be true for every money manager out there. Meanwhile, your after-fee, after-tax return is mediocre at best while the market gyrates wildly, giving or taking away the equivalent of an entire year's expected return in the course of a single week and doing that repeatedly during the course of the year.

EMH feeds into a grander school of thought that believes stock prices vacillate randomly, at least in the short term. The fundamental folks believe that short-term prices move about randomly also, but they feel those moves go back and forth around the theoretical intrinsic value (impossible to prove, of course, given that intrinsic value is theoretical). The random folks simply interpret day-to-day price movements as the intrinsic value itself moving about, primarily due to the different interpretations of intrinsic value among different participants.

## THE INFAMOUS RANDOM WALK

A bit of history will help introduce Burton Malkiel's random walk theorem. In 1953, highly respected British statistician Maurice Kendall published an article titled "The Analytics of Economic Time Series, Part 1: Prices" in which he concluded that stock prices on any given day are as likely to go up as to go down and that share prices essentially moved in random fashion. As this did not sit particularly well with some financial economists at the time, further debate and research ensued. Kendall, meanwhile, was knighted by the British government for his contribution to the field of statistics.

Twelve years later, American economist Eugene Fama published his PhD thesis at the University of Chicago, citing evidence from his own and numerous other academic studies that supported

Kendall's work, affirming that stock prices were unpredictable and claiming that they followed what is referred to as a "random walk," albeit one influenced by a long-term upward bias from economic forces such as earnings growth and inflation. Fama is credited with establishing the link between the random walk hypothesis and the concept of an efficient market. In published articles building on his thesis, Fama defines an efficient market as one in which there are

> large numbers of rational profit-maximizers which are actively competing, with each trying to predict future market values of individual securities, and where important current information is freely available to all participants. In an efficient market, competition among the many intelligent participants leads to a situation where, at any point in time, actual prices of individual securities already reflect the effects of information based on events that have already occurred, and on events which, as of now, the market expects to take place in the future. In other words, in an efficient market at any point in time the actual price of a security will be a good estimate of its intrinsic value.[3]

Fama published a series of random walk papers in the 1960s and 70s that are still cited by academicians today, though they appeared only in finance journals and were not generally known to the public. It wasn't until 1973 that Princeton Professor Burton Malkiel seized the opportunity to bring together the works of Kendall, Fama, and others on the random walk theory into a book aimed squarely at the public. In his book, *A Random Walk Down Wall Street*, Malkiel affirmed the notion that stock movements could not be consistently predicted, and he boldly concluded that, consequently, "Investment advisory services, earnings predictions, and complicated chart patterns are useless."[4] With a bit more color in his language than Fama, he further drove the point home by noting, "Taken to its logical extreme, it means that a blindfolded monkey throwing darts at a newspaper's financial pages could select a portfolio that would do just as well as one carefully selected by the experts."[4] Malkiel thus encouraged investors to buy and hold a passively indexed stock fund (these were just arriving on the scene at the time of his writing) to avoid the inherent drag on performance resulting from the fees and commissions charged by the pros to perform a portfolio-management role he claims to be unnecessary.

Intrigued by Malkiel's dart-throwing challenge (and no doubt looking to piggyback on the popularity of his book), the *Wall Street Journal* actually tested this premise, allowing its staffers to throw the darts. The *Journal* reported that, after thirteen years, the pros handily beat the dart throwers on both an absolute basis as well as a risk-adjusted basis, in opposition to what the EMH would suggest. Malkiel reviewed the results himself and said he believed the results were tainted by the *Journal's* methodology. Subsequently, an article in the *Journal of Applied Finance* argued that the findings as calculated by the *Wall Street Journal* were indeed biased, and on recasting them, he turned the results in favor of the dart throwers, thereby supporting EMH.[5] Is it any wonder why debate on the subject has persisted for fifty years?

### THE REALITIES OF RANDOMNESS

The statistical interpretation of randomness is not exactly the same as our intuitive interpretation. Malkiel defines a random walk as "one in which future steps or directions cannot be predicted on the basis of past actions. When the term is applied to the stock market, it means that short-run changes in stock prices cannot be predicted."[6] Thus, to say that share prices move randomly is not to say that there is a total absence of rhyme or reason and that Intel stock could be 22 today, 143 tomorrow, and 6 the next day. While the market is capable of sending prices on rather wild rides, there are generally valid reasons for such volatility, and there are market forces (i.e., bargain hunters, arbitrageurs, and the like) that keep price fluctuations confined to somewhat "reasonable" levels. The random theory also doesn't say that the market is just a big crapshoot and that you'll be lucky to make any money out of it at all over any period of time. Malkiel contends that the market effectively prices relevant new information into the price of individual stocks on a continuous basis, and since one cannot predict what the next piece of news or information will be, one cannot consistently predict any stock's next immediate move. He also implies that the knowledge of where a stock has been (i.e., historic price charts) does not enable one to project or predict its next move either because there is no dependent relationship to prior prices. It does, however, allow for the accepted long-term upward bias in stock prices resulting from growth, inflation, production efficiency, and other fundamental long-term factors. (Random walkers make no particular distinction, by the way, about where to draw the line between random movements in the short term and predictable movements over the long term—a fact that seriously damages the practicality of their theory for optimizing investment over time.)

There is much more to the concept of randomness than meets the eye. In fact, we humans literally don't even know what randomness looks like, according to Nassim Nicholas Taleb, author of the eye-opening book *Fooled by Randomness*. A professor, ex-trader, and expert on randomness, Taleb claims we tend to visualize randomness as a graphical interpretation or stream of data with absolutely no discernible pattern whatsoever. But randomness is full of patterns; to concoct supposedly random samples by removing all semblance of patterns, we actually induce artificiality to random data. As with the concept of infinity, the human mind simply has difficulty grasping the true consequences of elementary randomness. Taleb says that among other things, we underestimate the effects of randomness, mistakenly attribute success to skill and failure to randomness, and that "Our mind is not equipped with the adequate machinery to handle probabilities."[6]

In *The Black Swan*, Taleb also discusses the difference between true randomness and deterministic chaos, and he profoundly concludes, "In practice, randomness is fundamentally incomplete information."[7] To say that stocks follow a random walk is to say that one cannot input the last $N$ price ticks and have a computer tell us with a high degree of confidence what the next tick in the series should be. But if we knew the intentions and behavioral characteristics of all the parties who might trade a particular stock, then we might very well be able to estimate that next price tick. Of course, knowing everyone's intentions is impossible, but if there are common behavioral characteristics across large numbers of market participants, we might be able to use that knowledge to narrow the range of possible prices. More on this in Chapter 10.

## WHERE DOES A RANDOM WALK TAKE YOU?

As you might expect, having encouraged folks to dump their financial advisors, forget about price charts, and buy index funds, Malkiel's message resonated strongly with individual investors while alienating most professionals in the money-management business and vendors of market commentary or information. His book has been a national best seller and thirty-five years later is in its eighth edition. The premise did appear to have, for better or worse, a strong impact on the investing public and may have contributed to the rapid growth in the popularity of index funds as well as on the academic community, evidenced by the voluminous writings on the subject over the last fifty years. Nonetheless, fundamental investment research still pervades Wall Street, and the investment-management industry still thrives on the people and institutions that are willing to pay fees for active portfolio management, despite the fact that published statistics readily support Malkiel's claim that few professional money managers consistently beat the overall market averages after their fees are considered.

Ironically, the investment-advisory business has embraced index funds and their younger cousins, exchange-traded funds (ETFs), in a big way. After all, they offer diversification and are by definition indexed to a benchmark, and they reduce or eliminate the need to do fundamental research on individual securities. But instead of reducing their fees, advisors simply treat the ETFs like any other individual security within a larger portfolio on which they charge their standard overall management fee. In so doing, advisors save stock-picking time by utilizing an ETF in the client's portfolio while charging the client the same overall management fee as if they were picking individual stocks. And if that isn't bad enough, there is a small additional management fee inside the ETF that the investor must bear as well! This is hardly what Malkiel wanted to see happen.

While the central point about the random nature of individual stock prices does appear to have broad and proven validity, the theory is acknowledged to be somewhat overgeneralized, even by Malkiel himself. In his book, he notes that,

> In fact, the stock market does not quite measure up to the mathematician's ideal of the complete independence of present price movements from those in the past. There have been some dependencies found . . . but any systematic relationships that exist are so small that they are not useful for an investor. The transaction charges involved in trying to take advantage of these dependencies are far greater than any advantage that might be obtained.[8]

Experts, however, have disagreed and pointed to a number of specific anomalies that poke holes in the random market hypothesis, and these are far more significant than Malkiel suggests. In addition, Malkiel cited numerous techniques that are purported to aid in predicting stock prices from prior data and made sweeping statements about how each one has been proven unable to beat a simple buy-and-hold approach without citing specific studies that proved this to be the case. In fact, his book is curiously devoid of footnotes and text references to many of the studies he refers to in his arguments. In Part II of this book, I cite numerous examples of nonrandom anomalies, all of which are fully referenced.

Most importantly, Malkiel describes the random nature of individual stocks but makes no distinction between individual stocks and the overall market, suggesting by inference that if stock movements are random, then the movements of the overall stock market must also be random. On this note, I part significantly with Malkiel and the random walk theory.

The random walk school has many alumni, among them a huge number of people who first attended "listen-to-your-broker" school and later studied at the "stock picker's self-study" school but failed to successfully complete either program. The random school's only entrance requirement is that you have attended one of these other two schools first and have lost money or underperformed the overall market averages. The curriculum is very straightforward: you read Malkiel's book, and you invest money in at least one index fund. If you graduated from the random school, congratulations! You have learned how to achieve a mediocre long-term return without paying a management fee or as much in taxes to do so. The book you are reading now should add the equivalent of a master's degree to that knowledge.

## SUFFICIENTLY EFFICIENT

Both EMH and random walk are generalized theories that describe the stock market at a very high level. They are supported by volumes of research data, mostly buried in academic journals. Like most other general theories, if you dig deep enough into the details, you are certain to find flaws, exceptions, and anomalies, not to mention different interpretations of the same research findings. The academic community has been researching and writing about market efficiency, randomness in stock prices, and what constitutes rational market behavior ever since these concepts were first presented in the 1960s and 1970s, yet still there is no universal consensus. The very fact that so much study has been done over so many years says that there is sufficient ambiguity in the concept to satisfy both sides of the argument, allowing supporters to accept the concept as a general premise while at the same time allowing detractors to find numerous examples of exceptions and anomalies. More importantly, fifty years of debate has had scant impact on the way most professionals manage investments, except to accelerate the proliferation of index funds and ETFs.

One can readily see how opposition to EMH springs from the all-encompassing generalities used to state the theory in the first place. Efficient markets, for example, assume that information on stocks is available to all market participants, that they are rational decision makers, that information is instantaneously manifested into stock prices, and that prices fully reflect all known information at any point in time. This may be a bit too literal for folks who don't hear the news about stocks until they get home from work at night, who believe almost everyone is irrational, and who are convinced that they haven't got a prayer of learning anything about a company that the insiders and the professional traders don't already know.

Fama himself even acknowledged ambiguities. In one of his published papers, he states "It is unlikely that the random walk hypothesis provides an exact description of the behavior of stock market prices. For practical purposes, however, the model may be acceptable even though it does not fit the facts exactly."[9] Further still, Fama notes that statistical tests like serial correlations and runs analyses have corroborated the random walk hypothesis but that these tests might arguably be too linear and too rigid, respectively, to say for sure that certain types of chart patterns might not actually lead to timing decisions that would outperform a simple buy-and-hold strategy. This is a *very* important statement coming from the father of EMH and serves as a door opener for the chart work described in Part III.

With the stock market so broad and interpretations of random walk and EMH so loose, researchers can almost always point to some particular aspect of the market that makes their case either for or against efficiency and randomness. Proponents of the random walk theory, for example, tend to take a long-term, high-level, generalistic view of the markets. Their definitions allow for all kinds of minor inefficiencies (and even some major ones) to exist without technically negating the theory. The Internet bubble, for example, did not deter hardcore EMH adherents. They simply acknowledge it as a temporary, albeit multiyear, anomaly in valuations that eventually rectified itself. The S&P 500 went from 950 to 1550 and back to 950 in the three years from October 1998 to 2001. That's a 63-percent move upward in eighteen months immediately followed by a 39-percent move back down to the exact same level in the next eighteen months. During the same period, Yahoo! went from 10 to 110 and then down to 5. Malkiel responds to such activity by claiming, "Markets can be efficient even if they sometimes make egregious errors in valuation, as was certainly true during the 1999–early 2000 Internet bubble."[10] This makes me wonder just how extreme market behavior would have to be to negate the efficiency thesis altogether.

A particularly vexing issue for the EMH is that market prices are presumed to fully reflect all known information. There was enough backlash on this particular issue that Fama acknowledged the phrase "fully reflect" might be too rigid to apply in all cases, and sometime after he added clarification to the original theory. He resolved the issue simply by conceptually subdividing market efficiency into three categories depending on the level of information available: *weak-form efficiency* in which only historic pricing information is known and nothing else, *semistrong-form efficiency* in which prices adjust to all publicly available information, and *strong-form efficiency* in which prices adjust to all information, whether public or not.

In Fama's explanation, he says

> We should note that what we have called the efficient markets model in the discussions of earlier sections is the hypothesis that securities prices at any point in time "fully reflect" all available information. Though we shall argue that the model stands up well to the data, it is obviously an extreme null hypothesis. And like any other extreme null hypothesis, we do not expect it to be literally true. The categorization of the tests into weak, semi-strong and strong form will serve the useful purpose of allowing us to pinpoint the level of information at which the hypothesis breaks down.[11]

Also implicit to the concept of an efficient stock market is the notion that information on companies, stocks, or external factors that would affect the value of stocks is quickly and widely disseminated among market participants. If one thinks about how rapidly news announcements move stocks today, one would probably accede to a high degree of efficiency from that perspective. From a practical standpoint, individual investors don't have the luxury (if you want to call it that) of sitting in front of a computer all day long watching stocks or news—nor, for that matter, do most money managers and other professionals. But a sufficient number of traders, insiders, and stock followers do, and they are in a position to receive and act on information much faster than the rest of us. What's more, we (and the Securities and Exchange Commission) need to overcome our denial of the widespread phenomenon of people acting on information before it becomes public. One has only to watch enough stocks and their options to see that movements prior to public announcements are commonplace. Admittedly, much of this movement simply represents best guesses by the general market in anticipation of material announcements, but at other times it is undoubtedly due to information known and acted on by insiders or other privileged parties. Either way, the market has become quite adept at anticipating news before it is publicly disseminated, at least on top-tier stocks.

Ironically, the existence of insider trading makes the markets actually appear more efficient, implying that the market is smart enough to anticipate the next news item. Just because there is no individual or group that is systematically monopolizing and acting on inside information doesn't mean that there aren't constant individual occurrences. Inside information in securities trading is a fact of life, whether the blatantly illegal Martha Stewart–type or the less blatant but not any less illegal type that occurs all the time in public corporations. Tons of information leak out into the marketplace prior to public announcements. Much of it is hard to segregate in stock behavior as it is buried within normal trading activity, but you can see it far more readily in the options market, where spikes in volume and implied volatility can stick out like a sore thumb. This information gets built into a stock's price ahead of a public announcement, thus blunting the eventual move when an announcement is made. This may make the market look even more efficient since an efficient market is one where you cannot obtain an advantage by buying immediately upon news dissemination. Do not confuse an efficient market with a fair one.

Research that examines whether it is possible to act on publicly distributed information tends to focus on specific news announcements deemed to be of material consequence and then to see if these news items are quickly absorbed into the prices of those stocks. When they are, research concludes that the market is therefore efficient. Studies do not approach the issue from the other direction— focusing on the variability in stock prices and seeking to identify the news (whether publicly available or not) that caused such movement. This is not easily done because there is no way to determine exactly what public or nonpublic news caused a given move in a stock's price without polling each participant who bought (or declined to buy) stock during the price advance to ask why. But by ignoring all the variability in stock price movement that isn't necessarily attributable to a specific announcement, we are ignoring a huge amount of stock volatility that could potentially be exploited. According to Robert Shiller, "In 1989, David Cutler, James Poterba and Lawrence Summers compiled a list of the fifty largest U.S. stock market daily movements as measured by the S&P since WWII, and tabulated them against news headlines of the day. Most did not correspond to any major news announcement that would account for such movement."[12]

On the surface, the random market premise sounds logical enough, even if somewhat all-encompassing, and no doubt strikes an intuitive chord with investors who are constantly befuddled by the seemingly unpredictable gyrations in stock prices. In fact, with the monumental advances in information technology since the 1960s and 1970s, the market could well be expected to be a good measure more efficient now than when the random theory first became popular. In the 1970s, stock research was available only by mail or printed in the daily newspaper the next morning. In addition, some say the fact that we have a relatively efficient stock market is not an altogether bad thing. It is what makes our capital-raising system work as well as it does by providing corporations the ability to raise capital and the public with a relatively effective way to participate in the long-term growth of corporate America. But efficiency doesn't mean low volatility and doesn't guarantee that anyone will make money, and the degree to which our markets are efficient is still the subject of much debate. Most importantly, if the efficiency of our markets is far greater than the efficiency in most other stock markets around the world, how does that change investment strategy?

The debate about randomness and efficiency continues today in earnest, raising obvious questions such as, Why can't so many academics, authors, and professionals agree? Which side is actually right? What difference does it make either way? Why should we care about this debate? Where does it leave us? For many of the PhDs, and particularly the ones who support random walk and EMH, it is no doubt largely about intellectual pursuits and publishing requirements. The only real action is to use index funds over an actively managed portfolio. But for those who focus on ways to disprove the theories, the potential for actionable results is huge. If the market is efficient and random, then the efforts of thousands of advisors and portfolio managers is essentially wasted and the fees paid to them are unnecessary, as Malkiel suggested. But despite nearly a half century since this theory was brought forth, fundamental research is alive and well. On the other hand, if the market, or even specific aspects of it, are in fact nonrandom, then they are by definition predictable. And if predictable to any reliable degree, such nonrandom situations can lead to profits in stocks outside of the expected long-term returns they already exhibit.

Given the number of years already spent thus far on the subject, and the number of arguments on both sides, it seems this debate is likely to persist in perpetuity. For the purposes of this book, it is important to recognize that there are acknowledged anomalies in the random walk and EMH theories, and that they may be much more significant than previously thought.

## CRACKS IN THE RANDOM WALKWAY

Until the 1990s, the random walk hypothesis was widely accepted among academics and no doubt many individual investors. Most of the early research supported and affirmed the EMH and random walk theories, with little attention given to the anomalies. This is not unexpected as both theories acknowledge the existence of anomalies and irrational behavior but explain them away as self-canceling noise trading or as fodder for arbitrageurs, thus ascribing little importance to their overall effect on market efficiency. In addition, both theories convincingly reckon that if a meaningful anomaly were brought to light, then it would quickly be preempted or countermanded by the trading piranhas that constantly scour the stock universe for tradable opportunities.

In the 1990s, however, evidence began to surface from both academics and industry practitioners whose research identified specific situations where stock pricing appeared not to be random, not to be arbitrageable, and to persist. While perhaps viewed initially as anecdotal, such observations rarely came to light outside of academic journals. As more of these instances surfaced, however, academia came to realize that the irrational behavior of market participants may represent not just inconsequential noise but something more significant and systematic. Since the 1990s, the focus has taken on sufficient momentum to warrant the coining of a new catch phrase to describe it: *behavioral finance*. The new behavioral approach views the markets as generally efficient and for the most part random but with identifiable holes or imperfections that are caused by the imperfect structure of the market or the imperfect behavior of the participants. The implication of identifying nonrandom movements in stock prices is clear and potentially significant: such movements represent ways in which market participants might profit in the stock market from something other than the long-term trend.

Support for the behavioral case has been published largely by academics who have bucked the theories widely held by their cohorts to establish a new market model predicated on behavior. Their findings tend to fall into one of two categories:

1. identifying specific **market anomalies** in the price action of securities or markets that are inconsistent with what would exist in an efficient market, and
2. identifying ways in which **human behavior** deviates from the expected behavior of participants in an ideally efficient market and examining how that leads to market anomalies.

I've devoted a chapter to each of these areas in Part II. The approach outlined in Part III pulls together some of the aspects of both these perspectives with a unique spin.

## Can Stocks Be Random but Markets Not?

Even the random walkers acknowledge that while stock prices are random in the short run, they do have a valid upward bias over the long term. That means they are not totally random after all from a long-term perspective. While the movement of individual stocks supports the random hypothesis, the markets imply something very different.

The market exhibits decidedly nonrandom characteristics in both the short- and long-term. Therefore, it may be possible for the action of individual stocks to be predominantly random, while predictable patterns exist at the market level.

There is precedent in physics for such a phenomenon. At the subatomic level, it is acknowledged that the rules of quantum physics apply and randomness exists with regard to particle activity. Such randomness, however, does have constraints imposed by natural forces. That is to say, if there are two electrons associated with a single atom, they may move about randomly but exist within a confined domain (i.e., one cannot be observed in a laboratory in Los Angeles while the other exists in Cleveland). Thus, they exhibit a *contained randomness*. Yet as we observe macroscopic phenomena, even though made up of subatomic particles, that randomness of activity disappears and classic physics rules apply.[13] This is analogous to stocks and markets: stocks move randomly within given parameters, but when aggregated they display nonrandom characteristics not evident in the individual components. Kendall, the original British statistician who first observed that stocks were random, apparently saw something similar. In his 1953 paper, he notes, "There is experimental evidence and theoretical support for the belief that aggregative index numbers might behave more systematically than their components. This might be due to the reduction of the random elements by averaging and the consequent emergence of systematic constituents."[14]

There are at least several intuitive arguments that support this contention:

1. Investment focus has long since drifted away from individual stocks and toward the market as a whole, whose performance is measured by the major indexes such as the Dow Jones Industrial Average, the Nasdaq, the S&P 500, the Russell 2000, and a number of others. Portfolios are benchmarked against market indexes, and performance comparisons all relate to those benchmarks. Indeed, the only purpose of picking individual stocks in the first place is to achieve the long-term returns offered by stocks as a group.

2. Modern portfolio theory has created a broader perspective on what investment portfolios should consist of and considers stocks to be just one of many available asset classes. Equities now commonly sit alongside other classes of assets such as real estate, precious metals, commodities, emerging market stocks and debt, and other "alternative" investments. This higher-level focus on asset class further reduces the emphasis on individual stock selection.

3. Numerous tradable securities now exist in the form of ETFs to represent indexes of all kinds. Market participants can much more easily play the market as a whole now without even having to select individual stocks.

4. Arbitrage, particularly between the major indexes and their respective futures derivatives, has become an enormous phenomenon, aided by big money and push-button program trades that can acquire or unload a basket of stocks in an instant. In such activity, the fundamental values of the underlying stocks are completely irrelevant. All that matters is the value of the spread between the futures and the collective basket of stocks.

In the world of individual stocks and stock markets, the tail now wags the dog. Trading the market has different characteristics, different players, and different modus operandi than trading individual stocks. Stocks exhibit random characteristics in the short term; markets actually exhibit nonrandom characteristics in both the short and long term. This is an important distinction that few people have addressed, but one that leads to the conclusion that the stock market is indeed far from random.

### Chapter Notes

1. Eugene F. Fama, "Efficient Capital Markets: A Review of Theory and Empirical Work," *Journal of Finance*, 25(2) (May 1970): p. 388.
2. Jacqueline Doherty, "What's with Those Rose-Colored Glasses?" *Barron's*, Nov. 3, 2008.
3. Eugene F. Fama, "Random Walks in Stock Market Prices," *Financial Analysts Journal*, 21(5) (Sept.–Oct. 1965): pp. 55–59.

4. Burton G. Malkiel, *A Random Walk Down Wall Street* (New York: W. W. Norton & Co., 2003), p. 24.

5. Gary E. Porter, "The Long-Term Value of Analysts' Advice in the Wall Street Journal's Investment Dartboard Contest," *Journal of Applied Finance*, Oct. 1, 2004.

6. Nassim Nicholas Taleb, *Fooled by Randomness* (New York: Random House, 2004), p. xlii.

7. Nassim Nicholas Taleb, *The Black Swan* (New York: Random House, 2007), p. 198.

8. Malkiel, op. cit.

9. Fama, "Random Walks," op. cit.

10. Malkiel, op. cit., p. 151.

11. Fama, "Efficient Capital Markets," op. cit., p. 388.

12. Robert J. Shiller, *Irrational Exuberance* (New York: Doubleday, 2005), p. 91.

13. Credit is due to PhD physicist Ravi Gomatam, head of the Bhaktivedanta Institute of Mumbai and Berkeley, for insight on this concept.

14. M. G. Kendall and A. Bradford Hill, "The Analytics of Economic Time Series, Part 1: Prices," *Journal of the Royal Statistical Society*, Series A (General), 116(1) (1953): pp. 11–34.

# Market Timing   **5**

---

*The great lie foisted on investors is that it's always a good time to buy stocks.*[1]

STEVEN M. SEARS, Barron's

T HE CONCEPT OF market timing suffers a decidedly negative reputation in the investment world sustained by Wall Street, news media, academia, government regulatory bodies, and most major industry constituents. The overriding perception is that it is not possible to time the market successfully and consistently, and it is therefore senseless, if not downright irresponsible, to try. The moderate viewpoint holds that one will lose money or reduce overall investment performance in the attempt; in the extreme, there are those who believe it is actually bad for the markets. On the notion of losing money, I heartily agree. Trying to time the market using fundamental factors—or worse, hunch—is destined to be a losing proposition. But on the idea that market timing is bad or that there might not be valid tools available for making such decisions, I couldn't disagree more. Universally held opinions, especially those borne of ignorance, have been proven wrong throughout history.

Despite the frequent appearance of the term in the media and in investment literature, different interpretations of *market timing* abound. An Internet search will turn up as many different definitions as there are sources. Some specifically point to market timing as the activity that made headlines in the mutual fund industry several years ago when fund companies allowed some investors to purchase fund shares at net asset value after the close of trading on U.S. stocks.

Announcements after the close or information from trading in futures or foreign markets enabled those investors to gain an advantage at the expense of other fund shareholders. The practice was banned and fund companies were fined. For lack of a better term, the practice was dubbed *market timing*, but that is not what the conventional practice of market timing is about.

A more relevant definition of market timing is offered by InvestorWords.com, which defines it as "attempting to predict future market directions, usually by examining recent price and volume data or economic data, and investing based on those predictions." This definition captures the two aspects of market timing that are most important: (1) that it is an investment technique based on technical factors (i.e., price history) rather than fundamentals; and (2) that it involves analyzing the direction of the overall market rather than individual stocks. Therefore, market timing is the process of developing or enhancing an investment strategy for stocks by determining the current and potential future direction of the overall equity market or major subgroups.

Market timing is frequently associated with and painted with the same negative brush as "trading," though you may note that the timing aspect does not necessarily imply a trading frequency but refers instead to the act of determining when it is an attractive time to enter or leave the market. A conventional, fundamentally driven portfolio manager who turns over a portfolio 100 percent to 200 percent a year (not uncommon these days) is considered neither a trader nor a market timer but rather a money manager. An individual, on the other hand, who makes a single strategic move to get out of equities entirely, even if only once in five years, is considered a market timer. A simple way to think about market timing is to say that any equity investor who does not remain fully invested at all times is trying to time the market.

You may also see market timing confused with *active investing*. Most investment managers would bristle at such an association because they consider themselves active investment managers by definition, and they would strongly object to being labeled market timers. Active investing is what portfolio and fund managers do.

If we do not choose to use a money manager, then we have ways to invest passively by creating a portfolio of index funds, target funds, or ETFs and holding them indefinitely without the necessity of continuous oversight. Active investing thus describes portfolios for which an investment manager (or the investor himself) continually monitors the portfolio. For investment portfolios that are held by individuals at discount firms or with commissioned brokers, some may be actively managed by the investor, but most are simply not managed at all. Thus, active investing has no particular relation to market timing.

*Market timing* is a term used widely by the mutual fund industry, where online access enables fund investors to move assets between funds or into cash with a few mouse clicks on any given day, regardless of size. This, in fact, is one of the primary features of most 401(k) plans now. Fund companies are compelled to offer this capability for competitive purposes but are not happy when investors pile in or out of equity funds en masse because it forces the portfolio managers to put large amounts of money into the market or to liquidate large portions of the portfolio within the same day, all the while attempting to retain the proportional integrity of the fund's overall holdings. This scramble by fund managers has been pointed to as one of the leading factors in recent times of large market moves during the final thirty minutes of the trading day. Many fund companies place language in their literature giving them the right to restrict people from making moves too often (i.e., market timing) if the portfolio manager feels it hampers their ability to effectively manage the fund. From the fund manager's perspective, they would love for everyone to just put their money into funds and forget about it for years and years. But to restrict or prohibit someone from taking their money out of equities on any given day is tantamount to a theater operator refusing to make exit doors big enough to handle the theater's audience in the event of a fire.

As a bottoms-up approach to investing, fundamental analysis, by its very nature, cannot be used to determine overall market direction. For that, investors must turn to either general economics or some type of technical analysis. Since Wall Street has been loathe to embrace technical analysis, brokerage firms offer only a general economic overlay to their investment recommendations. General economics are helpful in understanding the big picture of market direction but are hardly precise or specific enough to call market turns or suggest that a trend might be about to change. Consequently, the result of Wall Street's economic overviews are little more than slight changes to recommended asset allocations between equities and bonds or cash (explored in more detail below). From my perspective, the idea that one must always remain fully invested in stocks is bogus and self-serving, reflecting naïve notions propagated by Wall Street and fueled by its managers' unwillingness to employ technical methodologies. The notion that there are certain times where it is more opportunistic to be invested in stocks and certain times when it may not be is a valid one and can be critical to long-term investment success. Regardless of how one determines when or how often such times occur, we should all have the right to make that determination for ourselves and to maximize our own wealth by buying what we want to buy when we feel it is opportune to do so.

## FORGIVE ME FOR I HAVE TIMED

From a commonsense perspective, there is no reason why the timing of investments placed in the stock market shouldn't be an integral aspect of investment strategy or can't be used to develop an investment strategy strictly on that basis. If it is an acceptable practice to move in and out of individual stocks on a continual basis, then why should it be unacceptable to move in and out of equities in aggregate as well? Why must we hunker down in defensive stocks (i.e., those expected to decline less) during the weak parts of the business cycle (and particularly during periods of contraction) when being out entirely might be a better choice? Why should we feel obligated to remain invested? Were people who sold Internet stocks before their peak or who exited the market entirely doing something wrong or stupid? Should they have held all the way down because, in some perverse way, that serves our financial system better? Such thinking is ludicrous yet surprisingly common. The fact that Wall Street cannot or will not offer a valid technique for timing the market doesn't mean we have to follow their lead. Look where their lead has taken us.

All of us who buy stocks in the open market—individuals, funds, and institutions alike—are traders, not investors, by definition. We buy stocks under several naïve assumptions and expectations. One is that we believe buying stocks entitles us to a higher return than bonds, cash, or bank CDs during any time period; another is that we are actually investing in the companies whose stocks we buy. Neither is true. The secondary market for stocks is akin to a giant swap meet, and the exchanges are just that—places to trade equities. Unless you are an investor in initial public offerings (IPOs), your money does not go into the company's coffers. It is simply going to another party who is swapping out of something else. Even those who purchase IPOs are not pure investors because much of their money goes to buy out earlier pre-IPO investors, company founders, and venture capitalists. Those who invest in start-ups or private equity deals may accurately consider themselves investors in my view, but the rest of us should come to grips with the reality that we all play in the secondary market and are all essentially stock traders, regardless of how long we hold them.

That being the case, what purpose is served by remaining fully invested through thick and thin? From where did the notion come that says you have to hold shares for months or years? By adhering to that philosophy, people tend to become complacent and lose touch with the risks that exist in their portfolio. Some tend to assume that they will get a positive return indefinitely. This creates a serious dilemma when a more substantial decline sets in. Without a stop-loss (a value below which you decide in advance you will sell) and with an overriding philosophy that is committed to a long-term buy-and-hold strategy, an investor will inevitably ride the downturn. Eventually, when a decline exceeds prior corrections and takes on the tone of a more-prolonged bear market, investors become caught between the proverbial rock and a hard place. (Remember, if you wait for the economists or the government to officially pronounce a recession, the decline will already have inflicted most of its damage.) Risk and tax aversion cause many people to freeze at this stage. Ultimately, they are forced to sell by their inability to withstand the pain of further loss. Investors have long been chided by the money-management folks for their tendency to panic at the wrong time and sell at what turns out to be market bottoms. In fact, it is widely held that markets don't turn back up from steep declines until there has been a pronounced capitulation, though that is of little consolation to the investors who simply couldn't stand to lose any more. But it is the very notion of holding on forever that creates the scenario by which people eventually sell when the pain is simply too great to bear.

To be sure, there are economic incentives to holding on to stocks. Higher turnover generates higher transaction costs, which create a drag on portfolio performance. As for proof that heavier trading negatively affects returns, a study by professors Brad Barber and Terrance Odean demonstrated that, "[of] 66,465 households with accounts at a large discount broker between 1991 and 1996, those that traded the most earned an annual return of 11.4 percent, while the market returns (were) 17.9 percent."[2] Also, tax rates are less favorable for short-term gains, and if you hold long enough, it is possible to avoid capital gains altogether by donating stocks with unrealized gains to heirs or charities. The decision to sell stocks, therefore, has considerable economic implications. Why can't we just let the economics dictate whether buying or selling stocks makes sense at any particular time? If timing the market proves advantageous to us even after costs and taxes are considered, what logical reason says we shouldn't do it?

## WALL STREET CAN'T TIME

Wall Street's answer to the last question is simply that you will lose money trying to time the market because it can't be done successfully. The primary reason they say that, of course, is because timing cannot be effectively practiced in an environment driven by fundamentals. Market timing based on technical factors would represent a monumental conflict with fundamental stock picking. The very essence of fundamental analysis is to pick stocks that are supposedly undervalued without regard for timing considerations, while the essence of technical analysis is to use historic prices without regard for fundamentals. The industry cannot easily justify decisions under both scenarios. If you move in and out of stocks or sectors based on fundamentals, regardless of time horizon, you are considered an astute financial manager. But, if you move in and out based on technical analysis (i.e., charts and price patterns), in Wall Street's eyes you are committing sacrilege. The view of most in the professional investment community is that technical analysis is tantamount to voodoo.

There is another very important reason why Wall Street will not engage or support market timing. Market timing is not considered a prudent way of managing money or an acceptable practice for financial fiduciaries. In the eyes of the courts and the regulators, the idea of taking a client to 100-percent equities in a managed account is considered perfectly acceptable (at least for more aggressive accounts), but the idea of taking any client portfolio, however conservative, to 100-percent cash—even in the midst of a disastrous market move—is considered imprudent. What that means to a portfolio manager, fund manager, and fee-based advisor or trust officer is that, at the very least, they would get their hands slapped by regulators for doing so. Worse, however, should they protect a client from a market disaster by completely pulling out of equities, and the market subsequently recover while the client is still sitting in cash, they could be sued by the client, and the client would likely win. Consequently, the penalty in lost business or legal exposure for trying to time the market and being wrong is far worse than the penalty for keeping you fully invested during a downturn, which receives no rebuke whatsoever.

Wall Street firms want us to accept that there is never a bad time to invest in stocks—that it's only a question of what stocks to buy and what the mix should be between equities and fixed-income securities. Their standard response to the idea of timing the market is to point out that had you been out of stocks on even a few of the biggest up days during the year, your annual return would materially have suffered, and since you don't know when those big up days will occur, it is unwise to be out of the market for any length of time at all. Wall Street, of course, has had decades to perfect its pitch. Its managers say this because they don't have the means to determine when those days are and they don't want the responsibility of guessing. In that sense, they're right, but the logic works both ways. Being out of the market on the two or three biggest down days could significantly enhance your annual performance (taxes notwithstanding). Furthermore, timing is not about picking those two to three extreme days each year in either direction—it's about picking periods of time from weeks to even months during which it may be attractive or counterproductive to own stocks. Extreme days don't tend to come out of nowhere. They tend to be part of a concerted move, and most of the market's biggest up days represent bounce-back rallies within major declines. Brokers cannot respond in any other way except to tell you that timing is hazardous. They simply cannot take on the responsibility for timing decisions because they have no mechanism for doing so, and their downside is less when you remain invested than when they put you in cash. Sorry, but your downside is less relevant.

Interestingly, this attitude comes from the very same industry that used to thrive on the transaction volume it could generate in our portfolios. The industry has largely shifted to the fee-based model, and in that model more transactions mean a lot more work with no attendant increase in fee revenue, so heavy trading is discouraged. In addition, big brokerages are now emphatic about having their individual brokers out gathering more assets rather than sitting in front of a terminal trading for clients. As a result, even if they did have a valid method for market timing, they couldn't implement it.

## THE RISKS AND REWARDS OF TIMING DECISIONS

More or less the entire investment community says market timing is foolish and cannot be successfully implemented. Indeed, attempts to time the market can easily go awry and at the very least will inevitably place you on the wrong side or out of the market during an advance, stretching your patience or causing you to question your tactics. But timing doesn't have to be an all-in or all-out proposition.

The sheer magnitude of daily market moves offers us an opportunity for varying degrees of success, some of which actually reduce risk rather than add to it.

If the markets moved up glacially, without going up or down more than a few percentage points lower or higher in a given month, it would be a lot easier to accept the historic average of around 10 percent per year as a reasonable return. But when stocks are routinely moving up and down 5 percent to 10 percent in a matter of days, it makes us justifiably frustrated with a net expected return of that magnitude over the course of an entire year. If you buy on the wrong day, not just your entire month but your entire year's returns could be out the window. **TABLE 5.1** shows the annual returns on the Dow Jones Industrial Averages over a 10-year period compared to the total of all up-day moves and down-day moves in those years. While this is not meant to suggest it is even remotely possible to be in the market during all the up days and out (or short) during all the down days, it at least demonstrates how little much of the market's total movements are captured over the course of a year by a straight buy-and-hold philosophy.

Table 5-1   Total Up Day and Down Day Returns for the Dow Over Ten Years

| Year | Total Absolute Price Movement (%) | | | Annual Return for the Year (%) | Ten Biggest Days (%) | |
|---|---|---|---|---|---|---|
| | Up Days | Down Days | All Days | | Up | Down |
| 2008 | 186.9 | 223.3 | 410.2 | −33.8 | 60.5 | 60.8 |
| 2007 | 85.7 | 78.7 | 164.4 | 6.4 | 20.1 | 24.7 |
| 2006 | 66.1 | 50.5 | 116.6 | 16.3 | 15.2 | 14.7 |
| 2005 | 64.7 | 64.2 | 128.9 | −.6 | 14.4 | 13.4 |
| 2004 | 68.1 | 64.3 | 132.4 | 3.1 | 14.8 | 14.1 |
| 2003 | 111.9 | 88.5 | 200.4 | 25.3 | 26.4 | 22.0 |
| 2002 | 146.6 | 162.1 | 308.7 | −16.8 | 41.5 | 32.6 |
| 2001 | 120.4 | 125.5 | 245.9 | −7.1 | 30.6 | 33.8 |
| 2000 | 124.1 | 128.2 | 252.3 | −5.0 | 28.3 | 31.0 |
| 1999 | 112.5 | 88.7 | 201.2 | 25.2 | 22.8 | 20.9 |
| **Averages** | 108.7 | 107.4 | 216.1 | 2.5 | 27.4 | 26.8 |

This gives us at least some perspective on the ultimate potential of market timing as either a strategy unto itself or an enhancement to an existing long stock portfolio. The average year in the ten in the table had a total of nearly 109 percent in up-day movement and more than 107 percent in down-day returns. That adds up to more than 216 percent in absolute daily movements in an average year. Professional money managers, portfolio managers, and fund managers spend all their energies trying to beat the annual returns of benchmark indexes by picking stocks or sectors that will outperform, and a manager who is consistently able to beat the market averages by even 100 to 200 basis points (1 percent to 2 percent) after fees would be considered one of the top managers in the country. The table shows that there is almost 200 percent (20,000 basis points) worth of daily market moves during the average year (not even including intraday moves). If we expect an average of 10 percent (1,000 basis points) of return over the entire year, then there are 19,000 basis points of excess movement that we forgo with a buy-and-hold strategy. Enhancing returns with timing rather than stock picking would only have to capture 1 percent of that excess to rival the best stock picking available.

Looking at the ten biggest daily moves in each year, we can see that the 10-day totals in either direction are generally larger than the entire returns for the year (as in 2007, when the ten biggest up days totaled 20.1 percent, the ten biggest down days totaled 24.7 percent, and the entire year's return was only 6.4 percent overall). This tells us that avoiding even a few of the biggest days in the year can easily double the buy-and-hold return or potentially wipe it out completely, depending on which days you miss. On the other hand, it also suggests that we might be able to secure an entire year's return during a small part of the year and remain in a risk-free instrument the rest of the time. Yes, this is all theoretical up to this point. And, yes, one could miss return while being out or actually lose money if going short during a market rise.

## ASSET ALLOCATION AS TIMING

Timing has always been the Achilles' heel of fundamental financial analysis. Because a company's business is an ever-changing conglomerate of financial factors, fundamental analysis can do little more than take a snapshot in time of a company's value. For a privately held company, fundamental analysis may be the only way to realistically assess company value (or at least establish a reference value); in a publicly held company, the market can (and does) overrule the fundamentals. In fact, we all know that the market can become severely disenfranchised from underlying fundamental value. Classic financial analysis can effectively benchmark all companies at a particular moment in time and tell you what the most attractively valued stocks are on a relative basis, but it cannot tell you whether it is actually a good time to buy any of them.

Faced with this dilemma and the undeniable fact that the timing of investments in equities (whether intentional or inadvertent) dramatically affects overall investment performance, fundamental purists resort to the use of asset allocation as a proxy for timing. Basic asset allocation for most investment portfolios boils down to an allocation among equities, fixed income, and cash. Under the rationale of lowering overall portfolio volatility and optimizing portfolio returns, managers will allocate a portfolio across these three main asset categories, matching the allocation to the client's risk profile and secondarily considering the status of the market. Allocating a portfolio across multiple asset classes in a manner prescribed by modern portfolio theory (MPT) is the accepted way to maximize returns while minimizing volatility in the portfolio, but MPT does not suggest that managers change the allocations at will if they suspect that one asset class is more attractive at the moment than another. Nonetheless, many managers and their firms will change the allocations, particularly when faced with a dramatic swing in the value of either equities or bonds.

The cash component of a portfolio represents a drag on overall performance and is thus typically held to 0 percent to 10 percent. Any larger and the manager seriously risks underperforming both peers and benchmarks. In addition, managers also fear that any higher allocation to cash risks phone calls from angry clients saying they are not paying a manager 1 percent of assets or more to be kept in cash. (Ironically, clients absolutely should pay a manager for keeping them in cash when the situation calls for that, but many clients simply don't view it that way.)

Typically, the amount of a balanced portfolio allocated to equities is around 50 percent to 80 percent unless the client is extremely conservative and wants primarily fixed-income securities. In an attempt to add value and potentially outperform peers, managers who feel that market conditions warrant it will vary the amount of the portfolio that is allocated to the three asset classes. Usually, this is done on little more than gut feel. Worse, it is more often reactive than proactive. Few managers urged clients to decrease their equity allocation in October 2007, but many suggested that they do so as the market plunged in the ensuing months. Most of the big wire houses issue a single broad recommendation on the basic allocation between stocks, bonds, and cash to give their brokers and clients a sense of where the firms see things. But because the firms are issuing a generalized allocation applicable to virtually all of their clients, it ends up being a watered down guide that rarely varies much less than 50 percent to 55 percent equities or more than about 15 percent cash. What they were essentially saying is that equities or bonds don't look very good on the whole and clients should still invest in them but perhaps a little more or less. In this manner, the firms can implement crude timing recommendations without conflicting with the recommendations on individual securities. Unfortunately, brokerage allocation recommendations provide an extremely poor excuse for a timing strategy.

## DOW THEORY AS TIMING

Famous for his theory on the stock market's movements and for creating the concept of an index or average of multiple stocks, Charles H. Dow, editor and part owner of the *Wall Street Journal*, may well have planted the first seed of market timing in this country. Dow created the industrial and transport averages that still bear his name, using these indexes to illustrate his theory about the cyclical nature of the overall market for stocks, publishing it only in bits and pieces in editorials by the *Wall Street Journal* during the late 1800s. Twenty years after Dow's death, William Peter Hamilton collected his writings into a book called *The Stock Market Barometer* (Harper & Brothers, 1922) and further refined the theory for public use.

Dow saw the market continually moving in three simultaneous cycles: a primary cycle (a major bull or bear trend lasting at least one year and typically four to six years), secondary cycles (counter-trend rallies or corrections inside the major trend lasting ten to sixty days), and underlying fluctuations in day-to-day buying and selling. Dow postulated that the market essentially acted as a barometer (or what we might now call a *leading indicator*) of business activity. Inherent to his theory was that one could ascertain where the market was in the various cycles through his averages and use that as an aid in the timing of investments. In Hamilton's words, "It is essentially the business of a barometer to predict. In that lies its great value, and in that lies the value of Dow's Theory. The stock market is essentially the country's, and even the world's, business, and the theory shows how to read it."[3]

The idea that the market exhibits a recurring periodicity commensurate with the ebb and flow of aggregate business health, and that this phenomenon could be formally described, represented a groundbreaking revelation for stock investors. Dow's key message focused on the identification and confirmation of the primary trend, which represented a valuable leap forward in understanding the stock market. It also provided at least some kind of tool that could be used to determine when it appeared relatively attractive to own stocks and when it did not. Nonetheless, Hamilton conceded that, "The stock market barometer is not perfect, or to put it more correctly, the adolescent science of reading it is far from having attained perfection. But . . . it does discharge its function of prediction, when viewed over any reasonable length of time, with almost uncanny accuracy."[4] He further noted that while Dow's cycles suggested an obvious periodicity, the movements were not of equal duration, and that manipulating them into mathematically calculable and recurring cycles would undermine the basis of the theory and yield nothing usable.

A study by Alfred Cowles in 1934 used Hamilton's market comments (255 of them were printed as editorials in the *Wall Street*

*Journal* during Hamilton's tenure as editor between 1902 and 1929) to determine the effectiveness of Dow theory (or at least Hamilton's interpretation thereof) as a market timing tool and concluded that the theory underperformed the overall market during those twenty-seven years. While taking some of the air out of the Dow theory balloon for more than half a century, Cowles' conclusions were overturned in 1998 by a well-publicized study conducted by Stephen J. Brown (NYU/Stern), William N. Goetzmann (Yale), and Alok Kumar (Yale), and published in the *Journal of Finance*.[5] The study vindicated Hamilton as a successful market timer, concluding that Hamilton's market calls (posed as either long the market, out of the market, or short the market) did indeed outperform when calculated on a risk-adjusted basis and that Hamilton's market calls were correct more times than would be expected by chance. Hamilton's skill at determining when to short the market was particularly highlighted; he was determined to have been right twice as often as wrong on his short recommendations and was successful in keeping an investor out or short during several of the worst downturns during the period. Hamilton's strategy also entailed considerably less volatility than the buy-and-hold strategy for the period.

Once Brown, Goetzmann, and Kumar determined that Hamilton's results had merit, the team's natural curiosity led it to test Hamilton's (and Dow's) market timing technique hypothetically over the ensuing seventy years. This was a challenging prospect as it involved replicating a decision-making paradigm that was conveyed by Hamilton only through newspaper editorials and without the details required to know exactly what inputs led to those recommendations. To overcome this challenge, the research team employed advanced neural net technology to decipher Hamilton's original calls from market conditions at the time in order to make similarly conceived calls over the ensuing seventy-year period. All things considered, including numerous assumptions, the team concluded that a Dow theory approach would conceivably have matched or beaten a buy-and-hold strategy during that time and with as much as one-third less volatility. This may not necessarily send portfolio managers scurrying en masse to the *Wall Street Journal* archives for

Peter Hamilton's writings, but it makes a strong advocacy statement for the potential of market timing. The research team members themselves admit that the results do put a wedge in the ideological thinking surrounding efficient markets and the ability to predict the markets from past price data.

## TREND FOLLOWING AS TIMING

The simple premise behind the work of Charles Dow and Peter Hamilton is that the stock market alternates through recurring periods of time in which the general direction of the market either favors being invested, being short, or being parked in cash. Knowing where the market was during any of these three scenarios could enable an investor to ride the overall market movement using a basket of stocks without the need to continually evaluate the underlying fundamentals of individual securities. The objective of any timing methodology on the market hasn't changed much since then—that being the determination of opportune points in time as long, short, or out of the market. What has changed is that there are far more sophisticated tools and techniques available to determine when those opportune points arise, computers to help us make those evaluations in real time, and a host of new securities available such as index funds and ETFs that allow investors not only to get in or out of the market via a single transaction but also to effect a short position or a leveraged long or short position in a single transaction. We also now have low transaction costs and nontaxable accounts, like individual retirement accounts and 401(k)s, that further enhance the environment for market-timing strategies.

The basis of most market-timing strategies is the identification of a trend or cycle in stock prices that can be used to identify decision points for going long, short, leveraged long or short, or hedged long or short—or being out entirely and parked in cash. That is also, in essence, what constitutes the practice known as *trend following*, which is widely used in trading individual stocks and commodities. As Dow and Hamilton discovered, and as anyone now can easily see from price charts readily available on the Internet, it is difficult to argue that both individual stocks and the market as a whole tend to exhibit a rhythmic pattern of ebb and flow in price, regardless of what time scale one uses. Longer periods of time (i.e., weeks, months, or years) show more pronounced directional movements that are typically construed to be "trends," though trend analysis can be conducted in any time frame (and I will show later that even charts displaying five-minute price readings can be extremely revealing of price trends). The very heart of technical analysis is the identification and evaluation of these price trends, and there are a number of commonly used techniques for this purpose: candlestick charts, Bollinger bands, Donchian channels, moving averages, Elliott waves, and others. The determination of what actually constitutes a trend is somewhat unique to the methodology employed, but the objective is the same—the timing of buys and sells in accordance with the identified trends. Thus, market timing may also be considered trend following applied to the overall market.

## TIME CYCLES AND ELLIOTT WAVES

Numerous technical aids are used to make investment decisions within the context solely of time and price and are described in books on technical analysis. These include customized market cycles such as Gann and Kondratiev, momentum oscillators, stochastics, and Fibonacci series. One that deserves special mention is Elliott wave analysis.

Originally identified by and thus named after R. N. Elliott, Elliott wave analysis has been applied to stocks and popularized largely through books, newsletters, and articles written by Robert Prechter. While the concept behind the wave principle is essentially mathematic, it can be applied in many different disciplines, and Prechter is the impetus behind its successful application to the financial markets. What makes Prechter so unique is that he is neither a mathematician nor an engineer but holds a degree in psychology. His psychology background enabled him to develop links between the action of the stock market and social phenomena, thereby creating his own uniquely branded science that he terms *socionomics*. We know the term by its academic cousin—behavioral finance.

The wave principle, as interpreted by Prechter, describes the ebb and flow of financial markets in terms of primary waves, secondary waves, and corrective waves in much the same context as Charles Dow visualized them only with more degrees (i.e., sizes or amplitude) of waves along with a number of formal rules that govern the nature and configuration of the waves. Like Dow's theory, Elliott waves present us with a method of timing the market that can be used independently or as a guide for making other investments. As expected, there is no love lost between Bob Prechter and the Wall Street community, but the financial media has noted him at different times for being among the extremely few prognosticators to accurately warn of the crash of 1987 and the Internet implosion. As of the fall of 2008, Prechter also gets credit for predicting the 2008 decline, and his long-term forecast—one that will certainly not win him the optimist-of-the-year award—says that we have seen the peak in equities and that the Dow Jones Industrial Average will eventually bottom at a small fraction of its current value in the middle of this century. Right or wrong, Prechter remains one of the very few people in the financial world who has been willing to go out on a limb based on a market-timing methodology and who sees the relationship between human behavior and that of the market.

## TIMING AS INVESTMENT STRATEGY

While I have attempted in this chapter to remove the negative connotations of market timing and reestablish it as a credible tool that can be used to augment existing investment strategy, to aid in decision making, or be developed into a strategy of its own, I neither sanction market timing for everyone nor claim that it is a "system" for surefire success. Wall Street may be overly biased against market timing, but its warnings about losing money or reducing performance through attempts to time the market are well founded. Timing the market on a reactive basis and without the aid of a formal tool is likely to be a losing proposition, and no tool is capable of hitting precise tops or bottoms, so market timing will never be perfect. For that matter, we know that using fundamental analysis is rather imperfect as well. Even if you do believe that there are pockets of predictability in the great game of stocks, there is more randomness than we might care to admit.

Every technique for trading stocks, bar none, has weaknesses and will err with some unpredictable frequency.

From a risk perspective, using a simple timing mechanism to be either long equities or long cash will actually reduce the risk of a portfolio. If you are in cash when the market rises, you may certainly underperform, but over the course of any given year, a partially in, partially out approach lessens volatility over an always-long portfolio. Adding a hedged long component (i.e., hedging instead of going completely to cash) also lowers volatility. Shorting, or adding leveraged positions in either direction, will add volatility. Thus, market timing may add or reduce portfolio risk, depending on the approach.

Given the amount of price movement in the market relative to the expected returns we hope to extract from long-only strategy, timing may present a substantial opportunity. As the Brown, Goetzmann, and Kumar team concluded, market timing (even as crudely implemented by pioneers like Dow and Hamilton) bears further consideration. We know pretty well by now what the outcome will be with buy-and-hold strategies, and we know that the incremental returns from an astute stock-picking strategy are illusive. Rather than attempt to compete against tens of thousands of other investors, portfolio managers, advisers, and the like, all trying to pick stocks, it might make a lot more sense to focus on when it might be advantageous not to be in stocks at all.

### CHAPTER NOTES

1. Steven M. Sears, "Who Knows What's Next for This Market," *Barron's*, August 21, 2008.
2. Brad Barber and Terrance Odean, "Trading is Hazardous to Your Wealth: The Common Stock Investment Performance of Individual Investors," *Journal of Finance*, 40(2) (April 2000): pp. 773–806.
3. William Peter Hamilton, *The Stock Market Barometer* (New York: Harper & Brothers, 1922), p. 40.
4. Ibid., p. 53.
5. Stephen J. Brown, William N. Goetzmann, and Alok Kumar, "The Dow Theory: William Peter Hamilton's Track Record Reconsidered," *Journal of Finance*, 53(4) (August 1998): pp. 1311-1333.

# PART II

---

# Behavior, Behavior, Behavior

# New Thinking in Finance Isn't Financial

**6**

> *The market represents everything everybody knows, hopes, believes, anticipates, with all the knowledge sifted down to what Senator Dolliver once called . . . the bloodless verdict of the marketplace.*[1]
>
> WILLIAM PETER HAMILTON,
> Editor of the *Wall Street Journal*, 1922

THE PREVAILING FINANCIAL wisdom considers human factors to represent the static in the otherwise clear-sounding hum of an efficient, financially driven marketplace. It further holds that human factors are temporary, unpredictable, and self-canceling. Yet throughout the annals of stock market history, even the most revered financial luminaries have been uttering quotes like the one opening this chapter, acknowledging the impact of social mood and behavior on stock prices. Over the last thirty years in particular, a substantial body of work, including hundreds of academic papers and numerous books, has identified and substantiated numerous human psychological factors that affect financial decision making, and this body has concluded that these human factors are persistent, systematic rather than self-canceling, and potentially substantial. Yet almost nothing has changed in the way investments are managed in this country. Why is it that we are all in such denial over these important phenomena?

Part of the reason for this may be that, despite all the research on human behavior, few if any methods have been suggested for integrating this knowledge into investment management. Thus far, most of the literature has focused on the individual rather than on the markets, with experts suggesting that individuals learn how to recognize the effects of their own psyche on trading or investing with the hope that they might figure out how to avoid some of the mental traps associated with stock investing. This book takes an entirely different approach. I suggest that we, as a group, recognize that our behavior drives the market, acknowledge that it is our nature and that we are extremely unlikely to change, and develop investment strategies that embrace that reality. In other words, instead of trying to adapt our individual behavior to more optimal investing, let's adapt our investing philosophy to accept the influence our behavior has on the markets.

As long as human beings are the market participants, human factors in financial markets will be present. Volumes of research and empirical studies attest that they are permanent, ever-present components of a highly complex, dynamic, and interrelated system. Our emotions may be fleeting, but our psychological makeup has been ingrained over millennia. Furthermore, our behavior as a group is far more predictable than has been historically assumed. It is systemic, recurring, and predictable. While it is extremely difficult to prove, the human factors in the market may actually be the driving force rather than an inconsequential side effect.

Such thinking will clearly label me a heretic among traditional financial thinkers, which includes most individual investors, financial professionals, and many of my colleagues in academia. For some misguided reason (also linked to human psychology), people want to believe that financials drive the market and that our psychological imperfections simply get in the way. We may be grossly underestimating our effect on the markets. We laugh and we mock the human factors—heaven forbid we should hire psychologists to manage our money. We miss the point entirely. It's not that financials have nothing to do with it. Financials are the engine that powers the markets and impacts our behavior. But we are the drivers, and the complex interaction of the financials with our psychological makeup is what determines the market's behavior. How much Intel Corporation will earn next year is clearly a contributing factor in determining where its stock goes, but it's our perception of those earnings and how much value we are willing to place on them at any moment in time that determines the actual price of Intel stock and how it will vary over time.

Our attitude toward the stock market is hardly unique. We are just as complacent about things like the weather. We merrily roll along in our lives, gearing ourselves to the "normal" or expected weather patterns, ignoring the extremes that only come along now and then. Hurricanes are a perfect example. We do not build things or prepare things adequately for hurricanes, even in areas where they are known to occur. Generally, we have to suffer the devastation to wake up to the reality of its occurrence, and after having their windows blown out four times, some people might consider boarding them up. We exhibit the same complacency with regard to stock investing. Sadly, we are instructed and programmed to do so by the industry, government, news media, and most of the gurus we expect to steer us in the right financial direction. Their mantra is invest and hold, stick with it, and don't try to time the market. In effect, we're herded. We suffer from the delusion that says trading is bad, timing is futile, and selling short is un-American, if not downright immoral. We have been taught to be comfortable in our shabbily built homes, though we live in hurricane alley. The ultimate irony is that with stocks, the tempest is not an act of God, it is an act of our own making.

## THE MARKETERS WERE FIRST

It's uncomfortable for the average person to admit, but advertising and marketing folks have tapped into the inner consumer and identified myriads of psychic foibles that can be exploited. Their crafty slogans, provocative imagery, calculated offers, and finely tuned phraseology are all orchestrated to capture attention, create an emotional need to fill, and move the consumer to action. Marketing and advertising pros have been studying and utilizing psychological and behavioral characteristics for as long as those disciplines have existed. It's no coincidence that presidential candidates always wear red ties, white shirts, and blue suits.

A few people from financial firms have caught on to the predictability of human behavior, but paradoxically they are the ones in the marketing departments, not in the investment area. An acquaintance of mine retired from Citicorp (when that was its name) as a senior vice president in the company's credit-card marketing group. He shared with me how Citi spent tens of thousands on market research each year and then used the results to send millions of deftly crafted direct-mail pieces to the public. His group could predict response rates to the tenth of a percent. Similarly, they studied cardholder purchase and payment behavior and used that to make credit or rate offers to certain people to stimulate usage. It was an impressive use of behavioral science, and it showed that it's possible to quantify certain types of behavior when dealing with large numbers of people. With this in mind, how much of a leap is it to assume that stock-purchase behavior might be similarly quantifiable?

Another story to share comes from my graduate school days at the State University of New York at Albany, where I studied marketing under Dr. Thomas Stanley, an expert on financial marketing who later coauthored *The Millionaire Next Door* (Simon & Schuster, 1996) with William Danko. One of Tom's early research projects was for a bank in the Albany, New York, area. His mandate was to determine why people banked where they did. He interviewed a substantial number of people with the aim of determining not just which bank, but which branch of that bank people used. His result? The two factors that were most closely associated with bank and branch selection were convenience and the architecture of the building. Despite the banks' attempts to lure people in with rates and incentives, the main reason for consistent patronage of a certain branch office was about feeling at home in a building that was brick or stone versus one made of wood or steel.

While working at the New York Stock Exchange in 1978, I hired Dr. Stanley to help evaluate the results of a major study undertaken by the exchange to understand more about individual investors. Two thousand households across the country were interviewed. The data printouts from the study almost filled a room. This study was detailed in the introduction to this text. I asked Dr. Stanley to analyze the data and tell me what it said. He performed a multivariate computer analysis on all the data from the study (a process that goes beyond the answers to specific questions and allows the computer to look across all the variables to find out how the universe of respondents naturally classifies itself). After weeks of analysis came Tom's one-word response: "Psychographics." Wall Street had, of course, never encountered that word before. It meant that the factors determining how different investors behave are not related to how much money they had or where they lived but to their psychological makeup.

For an industry that had never before attempted to understand its constituents on such a grand scale, seeing the results of that study was the rough equivalent of being the first geologist to study rocks from the moon. Needless to say, Wall Street listened to the presentations we delivered and read the 150-page report we wrote but did nothing with that information. It was like offering sensitivity training to professional hockey players. Ironically, it was almost the exact same year that academicians such as Daniel Kahneman (Princeton) and Amos Tversky (Stanford) began prying into aspects of human behavior as they may be linked to investing and publishing the results in academic journals.

## ROBERT PRECHTER, JR., BEHAVIOR PIONEER

No book on how human behavior is linked to financial markets should ever be penned without recognizing the contribution of Robert R. Prechter, Jr. Prechter was an outspoken behavioral advocate and pioneer before many of the current authors on behavioral finance even got their degrees. To this day, he remains perhaps one of the only behavioral finance authors whose degree is in psychology as opposed to finance or economics, and he has written more books on the subject than anyone else.

Prechter's extensive work combines his broad-based psychological and sociological background with the works of R. N. Elliott, who—a hundred years prior—modeled human behavior and social trends into mathematical waves that represented how social mood evolves between optimism and pessimism. Prechter adapted Elliott's wave model to social mood and the financial markets, using the model to demonstrate how social mood causes stock market trends and economic performance in direct opposition to conventional thinking that holds that the causality works in the opposite direction. Prechter claims, "Events do not shape the forces in the market; it is the forces behind the market that shape events." In addition, he adds, "It can be surmised . . . that it is mass human psychology that is registering its changes in the barometer known as the [Dow Jones Industrial Average]."[2]

Prechter was given little respect by Wall Street, despite having begun his career there and having predicted the stock market crash of 1987 with alarming accuracy well before it occurred. Yet Prechter remains steadfast on the subject and has since predicted numerous other market milestones. There are many common links between Prechter's work and the conclusions drawn in this book. I salute Bob's pioneering spirit and for having the courage to stand by convictions that faced a veritable wall of industry and academic opposition. Those interested in the field should read his books, which I found to be far more readable than many recent works in behavioral finance.

### INNER IRRATIONALITY

In the world of efficient markets and random walks, irrational behavior is assumed to exist—but only among a small minority of uninformed investors. In reality, however, many of the things we do in the financial markets violate the standards of logic that are assumed to exist among rational investors, and we do them repeatedly and in large numbers. This is where the battle lines are drawn between those who study stocks and those who study human psychology.

Mistakes, missteps, and "irrational" trades are common to investing when they represent simple errors in processing information, errors in judgment, and inadvertent blunders in the execution of a predetermined investment strategy. Individual mistakes here and there, however, should make only a slight difference in an otherwise well-executed investment strategy. As widely accepted theory has it, the collective mistakes of millions of market participants tend to create nothing more than a noise factor that is exploited by professional traders and arbitrageurs. (Economist Milton Friedman argued that irrational traders will consistently lose money and thus not survive in the marketplace long enough to influence long-run asset prices.) But a recurring, systematic succession of mistakes or a significant flaw in the development of strategy in the first place can seriously affect long-term success or seriously affect the market's overall behavior. In the view of many noted academic experts, and supported by mounds of research, there are definitely pervasive systematic flaws in our market system caused by the fact that market participants are human.

Richard H. Thaler, a professor of behavioral science and economics at the University of Chicago's Graduate School of Business, may not be a household name like Buffett or Soros, and few people who don't have a doctorate in finance have ever heard of him. Thaler, nonetheless, is one of the foremost experts in the behavioral finance field today. The author of countless papers and several prominent books on the subject says, "I think it is now generally accepted that it is essential to understand how investors behave if we are to truly understand how prices behave."[3] While the importance of understanding the impact of behavior on stock prices may be gaining visibility, the research still has a long way to go to figure out exactly how that occurs, and the industry has even further to go in figuring out how to incorporate it into investment strategy.

People are just in denial, or have listened too long to conventional financial propaganda, or just don't want to believe it, but it's fact: we are the market. We are the "they" in the statements people make about the markets. "They ran that stock today just to shake out the shorts." "They must have known about that news—look at that drop in the stock price." "They" are us. We set the prices by our willingness to buy or sell, and the decision to buy or sell at a given price is only loosely based on the financials of the company. In fact, that decision may be wholly unrelated to the company's financials and may involve a host of variables of which we are not even consciously aware. It's no one's fault but our own. Maybe that's the biggest reason why we can't admit it.

More and more academics are acknowledging the human factors in investment pricing. Studies, analyses, and published articles are now abundant. A smattering of books has been published. But while some of this published material goes back almost thirty years, most of it lives in that rarified atmosphere of financial journals where only PhDs can breathe the air. Nothing has come out of Wall Street on the subject, and few people anywhere have incorporated any of the results into investment strategy in a meaningful way.

## THE LEFT BRAIN ON WALL STREET

Millennia of human evolution have shaped our bodies and our minds. So while we add a heavy dose of current education to our knowledgebase, we overlay that on to a psychological framework that is the result of thousands of years of human evolution. We are wired to think and act in certain ways, and we take this so much for granted now that we've lost our sense of how much that actually shapes the way we think and act.

The phenomenon is certainly not specific to financial matters. It pervades all areas of our lives. Psychologists, psychiatrists, social workers, counselors, and others are tuned in to that fact, but the financial industry is definitely not. Perhaps that isn't much of a surprise. Finance is a highly quantitative, black-and-white, computer-driven, left-brain world. The teachings are quantitative, the requirements are quantitative, and the people who enter the field self select themselves because they are quantitative thinkers. It's all very self-perpetuating. The trend in the last few decades has reached such extremes that it has created a hiring frenzy for "quants"—super mathematical, computer-savvy whiz kids (frequently, PhDs with backgrounds in math-centric subjects like physics) who are paid quite handsomely to develop the models that allow firms to build more complex products, manage proprietary trading, and develop sophisticated ways to arbitrage. The infamous debacle at Long-Term Capital, where quant theory blew up to the tune of $3.65 billion, doesn't seem to have slowed down the demand for such talent. A recent article in the *New York Times* cites one quant who says, "There are a thousand physicists on Wall Street."[4] After all, now that almost anyone who invests has a personal computer and Internet access, the industry has to stay several steps ahead to maintain its edge. As we now know, unfortunately, the actions of many of these quants exceeded the level of expertise of industry regulators, setting the stage for the mortgage market collapse and credit derivative implosion that cratered Wall Street in 2008 and nearly brought down our financial system.

Even if the industry were to acknowledge that human behavior affects financial decisions and therefore markets, it is at a loss as to how to build that into the quantitative logic base of finance and investment strategy. Admittedly, for hardcore left-brainers, dealing with human psychology and emotion is daunting and seemingly impossible to understand, much less predict or quantify. First, it is outside their mindset and therefore alien to their normal points of reference. Second, for financial folks, there is a certain amount of denial, which manifests itself as arrogance. Wall Street abhors the idea that they might have to employ human behavior to explain stock market action. They would prefer to just say that we sometimes do irrational things when we invest and leave it at that. It goes against their grain. You might just as well argue Darwinism to a creationist. The entrenchment of this attitude in the financial world is extreme.

Despite these biases, though, many aspects of human behavior, when aggregated over a large number of people, can indeed be quantified. Ask anyone at a marketing or behavioral research firm. Some in academia have caught on to this even while Wall Street hasn't. Hundreds of articles have now been published by PhDs who have studied the numbers and found oodles of evidence to support the behavioral premise.

## THE FINANCIAL VIEW OF IRRATIONALITY

Fascinating as they are, our brains are not perfect. Just as computers and calculators are designed for certain types of functions and are less effective at others, so are we. As we evolved, our brains became better at processing information in ways that were influenced by the survival of the species, not by the career aspirations of cavemen. While we think of ourselves as fast learners, our history with stocks and financial markets is barely a few centuries old while our history in caves spans tens of thousands of years. Financial prowess thus encompasses no more than an infinitesimal part of our evolutionary history on the planet. Consequently, it should not be surprising that our evolution equipped us better for evading large animals than for buying and selling stocks.

That does not mean that we as a society are totally ill-equipped to handle financial matters (though for many individuals, that is unquestionably the case). It means that our thought and decision processes are not ideally suited to that function. As a result, we tend to reach conclusions and make decisions based on imperfect reasoning or processing shortcuts that can (and do) lead to the kind of less-than-rational behavior that renders classic financial theory a less-than-perfect science. That is the concept of behavioral finance in a nutshell. If we as participants are not entirely rational (by scientific standards), then, likewise, the financial markets are not entirely efficient. If the markets are not entirely efficient, then they are not entirely random and if not entirely random, then they are at least partially predictable. To complete the chain of logic, we should be looking at the behavioral factors that make us less than rational to give us insight into market predictability.

## CHAPTER NOTES

1. William Peter Hamilton, *The Stock Market Barometer* (New York: Harper & Brothers, 1922), p. 8.
2. Robert R. Prechter, Jr., *Pioneering Studies in Socionomics* (Gainesville, GA: New Classics Library, 2003) (excerpted from "The Elliott Wave Theorist," August 3, 1979).
3. Richard H. Thaler (Ed.), *Advances in Behavioral Science—Volume II* (Princeton, NJ: Princeton University Press, 2005), p. xi.
4. Dennis Overbye, "They Tried to Outsmart Wall Street," *New York Times*, March 9, 2009.

# The Behavioral
# Phenomenon

# 7

*Economics is a social science, dealing with the behavior of individuals and the results of interactions where money is concerned.*[1]

WILLIAM F. SHARPE, Nobel Laureate

U NDERSTANDING HOW human psychology impacts behavior in financial matters and how that behavior affects the markets is a daunting task, but much progress has already been made. Dan Ariely sums up investor behavior quite nicely in his book *Predictably Irrational* when he says,

> Standard economics assumes that we are rational—that we know all the pertinent information about our decisions, that we can calculate the value of the different options we face, that we are cognitively unhindered in weighing the ramifications of each potential choice. We are presumed to be making logical and sensible decisions. If we make a mistake, the supposition is that we will learn from those mistakes and behave differently in the future. However, we are far less rational in our decision making than standard economic theory assumes. Our irrational behaviors are neither random nor senseless—they are systematic and predictable. We make the same types of mistakes repeatedly because of how our brains are wired.[2]

Harvard economics professor Andrei Shleifer, author of *Inefficient Markets*, states

> In short, investors hardly pursue the passive strategies expected of uninformed market participants by the efficient markets theory. . . . Investors' deviations from the maxims of economic rationality turn

out to be highly pervasive and systematic. As summarized by Kahneman and Riepe [Journal of Investing 1998], people deviate from the standard decision making model in a number of fundamental areas. We can group these areas, somewhat simplistically, into three broad categories: attitudes toward risk; non-Bayesian expectation formation; and sensitivity of decision making to the framing of problems.[3]

The everyday translation of that is that people behave differently as market participants than an efficient and random market would suggest in at least three general ways:

1.   People do not assess risk in cold, logical fashion. They tend to set up reference points for assessing gains and losses based on personal factors, and each person's reference points may be different. In addition, they exhibit risk aversion in the form of willingness to pay (or accept lower returns) to avoid risk even when the expected return of taking that risk is favorable. People are also prone to holding losers too long, thereby accepting more risk in existing positions than in those they would normally consider for a new purchase.

2.   People are not generally able to assess the probabilities of uncertain outcomes properly (in accordance with Bayesian logic) and thus systematically misconstrue the expected values of alternative actions. One aspect of this is the tendency to give more weight to recent history than older history in assessing probabilities of future prices (like putting little weight on the probability of a hurricane because the last one in the area was 1992).

3.   People will make different choices depending on how a problem is presented to them.

## HEURISTICS

This brings us to another term that does not exist in Wall Street's vocabulary but is highly prevalent in the world of human psychology—*heuristics*. Heuristics are the ways in which we arrive at decisions and the thought processes behind our internal logic. They are the subconscious rules of thumb, the neural shortcuts we take to make decisions in a timely fashion. The ability to process a decision to flee in time to avoid a stampede of woolly mammoths was a trait that had more survivability in our evolution than the ability to analyze their path in extreme detail and accurately estimate the chances of them trampling the ground on which you happened to be standing.

Heuristics are common to large numbers of people and thus govern the way we all think and act as a group. Heuristics that relate to financial decisions affect the way we as market participants perform our role on the markets. They are pervasive, consistent, ever present, and apply to all of us, whether acting as individuals or as financial professionals. Contrary to what many people may believe, financial education or professional training does not make one any less prone to the heuristics that we are all influenced by. While heuristics may be revolutionary to financial professionals, they are old hat to those who study human behavior. Thus, it is not surprising that the advancement of knowledge regarding the effects of heuristics on financial decisions (and on financial markets) comes not from the financial world but from the behavioral world. Accordingly, the authors of almost all published studies and conclusions on behavioral finance are people who were previously (and to this day still) unknown to the financial world or the general public. Interestingly, the two people credited most often with launching the behavioral movement with regard to financial decisions under risk and uncertainty are Israeli psychologists Daniel Kahneman, now a Princeton professor, and the late Amos Tversky, a former Stanford professor. While the names Kahneman and Tversky are inseparable with writings on behavioral finance, even today, some thirty years after their early publications on this subject and many volumes of confirming studies later, neither Wall Street nor the general public is likely to be familiar with their names or their contribution to the behavioral movement, much less use this knowledge in investment activities.

For that reason, included in this chapter is a highly condensed overview of the major findings in this area. This summary only scratches the surface of the knowledge accumulated over the last three decades and number of people who have made significant contributions along the way. For those wishing to dig further, consult the Chapter Note references for further reading.

### AMBIGUITY AVERSION

Investors prefer certainty to ambiguity in possible returns. That in itself is no surprise, but they are actually willing to take a lower expected return to avoid the ambiguity. The widely accepted standard in decision-making theory, first formulated in the 1700s by Daniel Bernoulli and refined in the 1940s by John von Neumann and Oskar Morganstern, says that a "normal" or "rational" decision maker (one who acts in his or her own economic best interests) will select alternative actions based on the *expected utility* (or benefit) of the outcomes. In simple terms, expected utility is calculated by multiplying the value of the utility by the probability of its occurrence for all possible outcomes and adding them together. Thus, an investment opportunity that has a 60 percent probability of returning $10,000 and 40 percent probability of returning $5000 has an expected value of (0.6)($10,000) + (0.4)($5,000) = $8,000.

But in reality, exact probabilities are rarely known with any precision. Ambiguity aversion occurs when choosing between an outcome with known probabilities and one with unknown probabilities. People will not only tend to choose the outcome or alternative with known probabilities when the expected utilities (using estimates for the unknown probabilities) are equal but also may even choose the alternative with known probabilities, even when the expected utility is less. In other words, people will give something up in order to have something more certain. It's the old adage "one in the hand is worth two in the bush."

Kahneman and Tversky published a paper in 1979 in which they stated, "Choices among risky prospects exhibit several pervasive effects that are inconsistent with the basic tenets of utility theory. In particular, people underweight outcomes that are merely probable in comparison with outcomes that are obtained with certainty."[4] The authors noted that since generally accepted utility theory was inadequate to describe decisions under uncertainty, they were proposing their own alternative model and calling it *prospect theory*.

By its nature, all stock investing is rife with uncertainty. Those of us who invest in stocks accept this uncertainty with the expectation that over time we will accordingly be rewarded with higher returns, and stocks historically provide a higher expected value over time than bonds or CDs. Many people choose to invest in bonds and CDs over stocks, however, despite the expected returns over time being lower; and during times of heightened risk, people tend to exacerbate their move to quality, artificially expanding the risk premium for items with less certain returns beyond what is historically justified. Ambiguity aversion relates closely to risk aversion (discussed later) but is distinguishable in the research and provides a separate effect. (In the extreme example of aversion to both risk and ambiguity of returns, for a brief time in October 2008, the flight to quality was so dramatic that Treasury bill yields actually went negative with the attendant rise in price resulting from panic-driven demand.)

None of this, of course, is meant to suggest that avoiding uncertainty is a poor or ill-advised strategy, only that investors as a group tend to think this way, despite rational investor assumptions to the contrary. In fact, as of December 2008, the returns of U.S. Treasury bonds over the last ten years have now exceeded the ten-year return on stocks and other riskier asset classes. Even over periods of time as long as ten years, the statistics of rational investing do not always bear themselves out.

### ANCHORING

Anchoring is a common and very important behavioral phenomenon. It occurs when people place a mental stake in the ground on a reference point that forms the basis of quantitative estimates such as stock prices. Psychologists have repeatedly found that when people are required to estimate something, they fix their minds on a specific point first and then draw the estimate from that reference. Estimates of price, for example, tend to be heavily influenced by previous price values for that item.

Anchoring can be an important factor in price negotiations. In buying a house, for example, we do not make a bid in a vacuum. We tend to anchor to the asking price and attempt to get what might be considered an attractive discount from that. A similar effect tends to be associated with the purchase or sale of a stock. For purchases, we tend to find a reference point from recent trading activity and base our purchase target on that. We then anchor our purchase price when considering what we would be willing to sell it for.

As with most heuristics, people are unaware of anchoring and equally unaware of the resulting price biases it creates. The anchor can be almost any familiar point reference—even one that is not related to the estimate being made. A classic example of this is an often-cited study conducted in the United Kingdom. People were asked for the last four digits of their phone number and then asked to estimate the number of physicians in London. Their estimates tended to cluster around their phone number: that is, those with phone numbers of, say, 2000 to 4000 provided significantly lower estimates than those with phone numbers of 8000 to 9000.

Anchoring not only results in the subconscious creation of a reference point but also can often be associated with a stubborn adherence to that reference that goes beyond economic justification. Ask an experienced realtor and you're likely to get a host of stories about how negotiations on million-dollar homes ended up breaking down at the end over a $75 light fixture. Fixation on the reference point also increases the burden on new information to move one away from that reference. This causes people to underreact to new information. A phenomenon called *price drift* has frequently been noted for stocks that make a dramatic announcement. The initial reaction, however substantial, tends to be followed by continued movement in the direction of the initial reaction for days or even weeks.

Another way anchoring applies to stock purchases is that people tend to anchor to a recent stock price or range. A typical example might involve watching a stock trade between 60 and 65 and thinking that you'd like to buy it at the lower end of that range, perhaps 60 to 61. The stock then trades higher, breaking 65 and moving to 66. Convinced that you will not see 60 to 65 again, you pull up anchor and end up buying the stock at 66 because you now believe 65 to 70 might be the new range. This may also explain why people will sometimes be too quick to buy into a falling market. They anchor to the previous high and then see current prices as an opportunity when, in fact, the current price may more accurately reflect new information or still even possibly be too high. This may also partially explain the power of countertrend rallies.

A more complex manifestation of anchoring may also be somewhat responsible for one of the most predictive phenomena in stock pricing: price trends or "trend channels" (discussed in much more detail in Chapter 10). In the same way that people are prone to anchoring to a fixed reference point, groups tend to anchor themselves subconsciously to a fixed direction and trend in both short- and long-term time periods. In so doing, they reference a trend's angle and direction and take action to buy or sell when the price gets sufficiently above or below the trend's base direction line, thereby perpetuating the trend. This may be linked to some kind of momentum bias and to herding as well. I have not seen any studies into this effect at all, and research on dynamic anchoring would no doubt represent a challenging task. Nonetheless, the empirical evidence is extremely compelling and forms the basis for my work in trend channel analysis.

### AFFECT HEURISTIC

To psychologists, our emotions, feelings, and perceptions are all considered to be affects. The *affect heuristic*, a term coined by Professor of Psychology Dr. Paul Slovic of the University of Oregon, refers to the way in which decisions are made on the basis of these feelings and emotions, even though we may perceive that we make such decisions on more objective and logical terms. Author and psychiatrist Richard L. Peterson, MD, characterizes the affect heuristic as the "'tags' that people place on complex judgments. For example, when asked about Google and IBM, an investor may feel (and subsequently think): 'Google is good and exciting,' or 'IBM is old and boring,'. . . These tags serve as simple and accessible judgments. The affect heuristic allows for quick decision making under conditions of time pressure and uncertainty."[5]

As Slovic and some of his coauthors have written, "This heuristic appears at once both wondrous and frightening: wondrous in its speed, and subtlety, and sophistication, and its ability to 'lubricate reason'; frightening in its dependency upon context and experience, allowing us to be led astray or manipulated—inadvertently or intentionally—silently and invisibly."[6]

Studies have also shown that when we tag something, that tag tends to stay for a long time despite our receipt of information to the contrary. These positive or negative tags distort our decision-making process. A candid example of how this manifests itself on a stock comes from an article in *Barron's* during the summer of 2008. The article pointed out that Oracle was doing really well but that its stock was selling at prices reflecting weaker fundamentals than were the case. The columnist had no qualms about sharing the fact that one reason why Oracle's stock was depressed was that a lot of analysts and portfolio managers openly dislike Larry Ellison—not because of poor management skills but because of personality traits. This is a perfect example of how decision making strays from objectivity in a manner characterized by the affect heuristic.

### AVAILABILITY BIAS

A common characteristic we share with our friendly personal computers is that our brains keep more recent information handier and more readily available. When recalling information, we tend to make judgments and decisions (especially the quick ones) based more on the available information than that which may be tucked away somewhere back on our mind's hard drive. Thus, when we form a judgment about something or assess the probability of an event or outcome, we rely more heavily on the references and examples that come to mind more readily. The most recent and most physically and most emotionally proximate information has the most influence. This has the effect of overweighting available information in decision making and biasing the resulting judgments thus rendered.

Available information also tends to color our views of the frequency or likelihood of certain occurrences. A nurse, for example, would likely offer a much higher estimate of the frequency of teen pregnancies than people who are unable to recall a single instance of teenage pregnancy among the people they know. This, of course, can also manifest itself in the stock market, where impressions of stocks or of the overall market may be incorrectly extrapolated from available information.

### BELIEF PERSEVERANCE

Talk politics with even your closest friends and you are likely to witness belief perseverance in all its glory. Once people make a judgment or form an opinion, evidence shows a marked tendency to stick with and defend it, even when presented with compelling evidence to the contrary. Beliefs persevere because people tend not to seek out evidence that would contradict their own beliefs; when evidence is presented to them anyway, they tend to put up a skeptical defense.

While belief perseverance often takes on extreme characteristics when associated with moral or religious issues, I have seen it take on similar strength in financial issues, particularly when people lose money and are searching for someone to blame (assumedly a common heuristic itself). During the great market sell-off of 2008, frustration reached extremes not exhibited in decades. Blame and finger-pointing were rampant. Long-held beliefs about housing, Wall Street, financial regulators, and government were severely challenged. Indeed, new beliefs were being formed that will undoubtedly stick with us for some time to come.

In his book *Predictably Irrational*, Dan Ariely notes, "Belief perseverance may provide a partial explanation as to why those who were initially taught the Efficient Market Hypothesis continue to believe it's an accurate theory when experience and research suggests otherwise."[7] A related heuristic called *confirmation bias* causes people to notice and even seek out information that confirms their existing beliefs and ignore contradictory evidence. In many instances, people can be so stubborn about their own beliefs that they mistakenly interpret opposing evidence as actually supporting their views.

### CONSERVATIVE BIAS

The bias toward conservatism is not about risk as much as inertia. Situations in which people tend to put a great deal more weight on base rates (the assumed probability of a particular occurrence) than they do on sample evidence (examples that might not agree with the base rate) are examples of such inactivity. In other words, like their stubbornness about beliefs, people tend to cling (or anchor themselves) to a base reference of some kind such as a long-term average market return even when new and compelling evidence suggests otherwise. Interestingly, when they do eventually react to new data, they tend to overreact.

### DISPOSITION EFFECT

Clearly related to anchoring and loss aversion, the phenomenon known as the *disposition effect* causes people to be heavily biased in favor of disposing (selling) a stock or other asset to realize a gain and against disposing to realize a loss. This effect overrides the underlying logic about whether it is appropriate to sell a stock at any given price with a bias anchored to the original purchase price. The disposition effect causes investors to book small gains much more than small losses and may be a leading reason why aggregate trading volume expands during up markets and contracts during down markets.

### ENDOWMENT EFFECT

Cornell economics professor and prolific author on behavioral finance Richard Thaler coined the term *endowment effect* in a 1980 paper to describe the fact that people often demand much more to part with an object than they would be willing to pay to acquire it. That is inconsistent with accepted economic theory that suggests the amount for which you are willing to buy something should equal the amount for which you are willing to depart with it (less perhaps transaction costs). In the words of Professor Jack Knetsch of Simon Fraser University,

> The evidence from a wide variety of tests is consistent with the suggestions of Daniel Kahneman and Amos Tversky (1979), and Richard Thaler (1980) that losses from a reference position are systematically valued far more than commensurate gains. The maximum compensation people demand to give up a good has been found to be several times larger than the maximum amount they are willing to pay for a commensurate entitlement.[8]

Thaler's early studies used simple coffee mugs and were conducted among students as well as business executives. The results showed that people were only willing to part with mugs if they received around $7, while they were only willing to pay around $3 to buy them. After ten years of studying the endowment effect and related *status quo bias* (the tendency to remain with the status quo over economically equivalent alternatives), Thaler concluded that "the endowment effect, status quo bias, and aversion to losses are both robust and important."[11]

The endowment effect likely plays an important role in determining how investors decide what to pay for a stock and what they are willing to sell it for once they own it. It may therefore play an equally important role in explaining the price movements of stocks, but it is arguably much more complex than the studies thus far describe. Experience with investors shows that the price someone will accept to relinquish stock once purchased is not fixed but dynamic and varies not only with the subsequent movement in the stock but also with time. For example, a stock is purchased at $30 with a price target of $40. On the stock reaching $40, the investor decides not to sell and establishes a new target price of $45. Likewise, should the stock initially sell down to $25 after purchase, an investor might decide to lower the initial target to $35. This scenario can often repeat itself many times and sometimes ends only when an alternative stock is deemed to offer a greater opportunity. Thus, endowment prices established for stocks are not necessarily a fixed price as with a hard good but will vary over time.

### FRAMING

Framing essentially refers to the biases in decision making that result from the manner in which the choices are couched. How something is presented makes a difference in many domains, and choices depend partly on the way in which problems are stated. Marketers, salespeople, and public relations professionals pay close attention to this human characteristic, addressing it through the all-important "spin" with which they present certain choices. A drug salesperson, for example, would expect a very different response from doctors if she said, "This drug has a 92-percent survival rate" than if she said "Eight percent of your patients may die from this drug." Numerous experiments offering people a choice of two options elicited different responses when presented in different context, and decisions to either purchase or sell stocks are similarly influenced.

The importance of framing is that it is not compatible with the theory of rational choice in which subjects are expected to be rational and hence unaffected by the context in which a choice is presented. In other words, a rational investor would choose to either buy or sell a stock based on the logical utility of that action and not the way the choice is presented. Kahneman and Tversky write, "The introduction of psychological considerations (e.g., framing) both enriches and complicates the analysis of choice."[9] In a broader conclusion about the impact of framing in the same article, they conclude,

> The modern theory of decision making under risk emerged from a logical analysis of games of chance rather than from a psychological analysis of risk and value. The theory was conceived as a normative model of an idealized decision maker, not as a description of the behavior of real people. . . . We argue that the deviations in actual behavior from the normative model are too widespread to be ignored, too systematic to be dismissed as random error, and too fundamental to be accommodated by relaxing the normative system.[10]

### GAMBLER'S FALLACY

As much as people want to disassociate investing from gambling, the similarities, particularly regarding the psychological effects on participants, are simply too strong to ignore. One of the similarities is the trap that gamblers commonly fall into in games of chance where they witness a streak or a run of some kind and wager the opposite under the misperception that the trend is now "due" to reverse. In simple statistical terms, it means that a person will perceive that after the roulette ball lands on a red number 5 times in a row, that the odds of a black coming next have increased and may now be in the player's advantage. In reality, of course, the odds have not changed one iota because of what has just transpired. Some betting "systems" actually suggest that players not only bet on black in the above situation but also increase (or even double) their bets each successive time another red comes up in a row. This may certainly work at times (just less than 50 percent of the time in fact) and theoretically could work all the time provided you have an infinite bankroll. Unfortunately, this is one of the many roads to a gambler's ruin. It's only a matter of time that the streak you're betting against outlasts your wallet.

Investors can easily see from historic price charts that stocks commonly vacillate back and forth over time (even though the behavior of stocks is not governed by the same laws of chance as a roulette wheel—and, in stark contrast to the roulette wheel, stocks are affected by the actions of the players) and apply a similar form of logic as above. When a stock's price departs significantly from some reference point like a moving average, they buy (or sell) under the premise that the price of the stock will now reverse and have greater likelihood of reverting back toward the mean or whatever reference point they have selected.

An interesting anecdote on this subject concerns Nick Leeson, the so-called rogue trader whose losses brought on the collapse of Britain's prestigious Barings Bank. Leeson lost a billion pounds of Barings's money in speculative trading. Ironically, his initial trades were not all that speculative and made money. But then, rather than take a loss on one losing trade, he went in deeper and with additional leverage (following the classic gambler's fallacy behavior). Continuing to "chase" his losing position, he ended up magnifying the loss beyond repair and bringing down the Barings institution.

## Halo Effect

The *halo effect* refers to the tendency of people to extend a virtual halo around a person, organization, or company that they like. It's similar to the way we tend to view our children—as good little individuals who can do no wrong (while other people's children are undisciplined brats!). When we like a sports team, we root for it, and we tend to see its players' performances through the bias of the halo we place around them. The same can happen with a stock, based on the investor's view of the company or the chief executive officer (CEO). The view that it is a "good" company or that it is doing well can bias or distort the view of its future prospects and whether its current valuation supports that prognosis. This may explain why the valuations of certain companies such as Apple and Disney that are well liked tend to remain highly valued relative to equivalent peers for long periods of time.

### HERDING

There is a notable tendency for people to emulate the behavior of others or to derive comfort by taking an action similar to that of a group they identify with. We see this in countless ways in social situations—in purchaser behavior, in parenting, and, of course, in the ultimate arena for social acceptance, fashion. Whether people replicate the action of others because it affirms what they felt anyway or whether they simply like to go where the crowd appears to be going is difficult to distinguish, but the effect is the same. It is called *herding*, and it is no stranger to financial behavior.

Investors frequently jump on the bandwagon when they detect other investors taking a particular action. Institutional investors and professional money managers are notorious for their tendency to operate within the accepted norms of their peer group. Even securities analysts, the folks paid handsomely to be smarter than us about the stocks they cover, exhibit the behavior. In *The Black Swan*, Nassim Nicholas Taleb relates a story about a published paper that scrutinized 2,000 predictions by securities analysts:

> What it showed was that these brokerage houses predicted *nothing*—a naïve forecast made by someone who takes the figures from one period as predictors of the next would not do markedly worse. . . . Worse yet, the forecasters' errors were significantly larger than the average difference between individual forecasts, which indicates herding. Normally, forecasts should be as far from one another as they are from the predicted number.[11]

Herding may stem in part from the common feeling among investors, whether individual or professional, that other market players are smarter or more informed than they are. Herding provides a certain comfort by association that can alleviate some of the pain of being wrong, and it may also result from the feeling of being left out or missing an opportunity. Thus, while some of this behavior may well be due to coincident conclusions being reached by many people simultaneously, studies have shown that taking comfort from the crowd, or herding, is partly responsible.

Another important form of herding is illustrated by those who "can't be left out" when others appear to be making money (no doubt part of what causes bubbles and manias). It is interesting that buy panics are at least as frequent as sell panics and perhaps even more so. This says that people rush to get either in or out for reasons other than simply the fear of losing money. Obviously, the fear of not making as much money as everyone else has a similar effect.

Another related phenomenon among investors is the *smart money effect*—the notion that certain people, institutions, or groups represent a higher level of investment acumen or are simply better informed and can be emulated for better investment success. Smart money people include high-profile investors, key public or hedge funds, investment-banking firms, CEOs of key companies, and media personalities. The herding concept is exaggerated and made even more complex by the smart money effect and by the number of pay-for-advice investment services and the plethora of ideas freely available from the Internet or through the public media.

The herding effect tends to be more visible in specific stocks or sectors over short time periods, where herding may concentrate buying or selling within a sector, thereby creating anomalies in pricing among stocks within that sector. But the more important affect of herding may be in the equity market as a whole over the longer time horizon, where it may be at least partly responsible for long-term over- or undervaluations. Actions taken by individual members of the herd may be rational but when aggregated, these actions can easily exaggerate price moves, feed volatility, and become irrational at the group level, eventually leading to a substantial overreaction or potentially a bubble.

Furthermore, I'm sure most of us would agree intuitively that bubbles are at least partially fueled by a herding effect and that the driving mood may be fear (translated as a form of greed) as much as it is optimism. Much of the real estate boom (or bubble if you prefer) of the mid 2000s was undoubtedly caused by people fearing they were missing the boat on the upside as opposed to those seeking bargains. The idea of overbidding on a house you know to already be expensive comes from the fear of not getting it rather than the joy of buying a cheap asset.

From a long-term perspective, I also believe we as a group have been deftly herded by the brokerage industry, money-management industry, and the media into the great equity-market corral with a reckless, one-sided abandon that fuels long-term equity-market overvaluations. Wall Street and its disciples are perennially in buy mode and very deliberately steer us in the direction of stock acquisition, even when the market is more than fairly valued. There is never a question about whether to invest in equities—a certain portion is virtually always recommended. Allocations may vary somewhat, but you can bet that if you bring money to a broker or money manager, you'll be steered into an overall equity allocation of somewhere between 50 percent and 75 percent with few exceptions. Being the helpless sheep that we are, we keep buying in, oblivious to the consequence that the market is absorbing too much new money and that equities might be getting overvalued.

As individuals, we are not even the biggest factor. The institutional investment community dwarfs us in size, and its herd makes our herd look puny. In recent years, there has been a concerted effort to increase the allocation of institutional money into other asset classes such as private equity and emerging markets, but that is offset by the herds of investors in other countries also coming in to feed on our markets. The latest craze, investing though hedge funds, only exacerbates the problem because that herd not only buys more equities but also buys multiples of what it has cash available for using leverage. Over time, more money simply chases after equities than is justified by the amount of new equities being created. Ultimately, the corral gets too full, the fences get trampled, and the entire herd runs for the hills. The pendulum then swings back the other way, with investors liquidating rather than buying until a sufficient overreaction occurs and the herders once again mount their horses.

Herding has become such a powerful force in the U.S. markets that it is not just a psychological phenomenon but actually built into our system. Laws concerning the prudent management of pension funds, for example, all but mandate that a significant portion of available funds be invested in stocks. Long live the herd.

### LOSS AVERSION

In the movie *A League of Their Own*, Tom Hanks uttered one of my all-time favorite movie lines when he said, "There's no crying in baseball!" He might as well have been an economist. According to economic theories, rational, emotionless beings are expected to operate with profit as their overriding motivation and to accept that losses are a fact of life and to take them when necessary or appropriate. But, in yet another clear-cut example of how we stray from the economic view of rationality, we have a severe distaste for financial loss. To say that we are averse to loss in a way that simply implies we don't like it grossly understates the power of this human emotion. Some studies suggest that losses are as much as twice as psychologically powerful as gains.

Classic economic utility theory says that between two alternatives we would choose the one with the higher expected utility, where expected utility is the product of value of some kind and the probability of receiving that value. Thus, if one has a 90-percent chance of winning $1,000 in a game of chance, the expected utility of that prize is $900, even though, in reality, you would either receive $1,000 or nothing. Given the choice between this bet and one in which there is a 100-percent chance of winning $900 (same utility), most people choose the latter as they would prefer the sure thing over the chance of winning an extra hundred dollars but possibly getting nothing. Yet when given the choice of a 90-percent chance of losing $1,000 versus a 100-percent loss of $900, most people choose the former, preferring to take a risk of further loss in order to avoid a certain one (again with the same utility). This was another finding of Kahneman and Tversky, winning Kahneman the Nobel Prize in Economics in 2002.

The impact of the psychological pain of loss is that it causes people to act irrationally in order to avoid it. Studies show that people are willing to take an additional risk to avoid a sure loss or pay to avoid a loss in the form of either placing a premium on an alternative less likely to sustain a loss or requiring a discount for an alternative more likely to sustain one. Paying (or overpaying) for insurance (whether on your house, car, or stock portfolio) in order to give yourself protection against a loss, regardless of whether it is financially sound to do so, is another illustration of loss aversion. Former Harvard economist Terry Burnham notes, "The strong hatred of losses creates perverse incentives. That is to take big, stupid risks with the possibility of avoiding the label of loser."[12] Consequently, the price of loss aversion shows up in the marketplace in ways that are inconsistent with rational economics, as in the example under ambiguity aversion of people purchasing T-bills at a price so high they actually ensure a small loss at maturity in order to escape potentially larger losses from stocks.

### MENTAL ACCOUNTING

In classic economic thinking, all money is considered equal. Ten dollars in your left pocket equals ten dollars in your right pocket. We humans, however, don't always think of it that way, and *mental accounting* is the term that describes this characteristic. For example, people typically divide their assets into different mental subcategories (let's call them "buckets") and assign different values of utility to the different categories. It is common, for example, for people to establish in their minds savings buckets separate from their investment buckets. Sometimes an investment bucket is further subdivided into a conservative investment bucket and a more-aggressive investment bucket. Money and risk take on a different meaning in different buckets, and the buckets tend to be nontransferable.

You may notice that the moment you walk through the entrance to a casino, the money in your pocket takes on a different value and changes back the instant you leave. On the way to the casino, you may squawk about having to pay ten cents more per gallon than you usually pay for gas. Inside the casino, you throw $10 or $25 chips on the table like you are pitching bottle caps. We mentally segregate our personal finances as well. Some of us get a 5-percent CD on

$30,000 in a savings account while taking out a car loan for $30,000 at 11 percent. Even worse, you would be astonished at how many people keep large sums of money (as much as hundreds of thousands) in checking accounts earning little or no interest at all or in savings accounts earning a few paltry percent. The money in the bank takes on a different mental utility value than money invested elsewhere. This may seem smart to us, but it is not a rational concept in the eyes of classical economics.

Mental accounting can go much further. Couples frequently set up his and hers buckets (plus separate ones for the kids), often applying very different utility to the different family member buckets. This may save (or break) marriages, but it's not a sign of rational economic thinking in the eyes of theorists. Complicating this is money that comes from inheritances or is accumulated in one marriage and then ported to another. Working in the trust world gives you a bird's eye view of the enormous complexities, inconsistencies, and emotional biases associated with money and families. Those in the trust and estate-planning worlds were probably not the least bit surprised when they learned that Leona Helmsley left $12 million to her dog.

Mental accounting is also used to separate buckets within the pyramid of wealth that we build throughout our lives. Generally, the more wealth someone has, the more concern for safety and preservation versus growth. Hirsch Shefrin, author of *Beyond Greed and Fear*, describes how people mentally assign money into "layers" based on different levels of security and potential. He cites an informal study that indicated as much as 80 percent of people may think this way about their assets.[13]

The concept of mental accounting can be interpreted rather loosely to accommodate the many different ways we assign value to money or investments. People even account differently in their minds for investments made in different individual securities. The same money invested in a biotech start-up takes on very different utility when reinvested in a gold-mining operation. The bottom line is that the way we account for money in our minds varies with numerous different variables such as time, level of wealth, life changes, and family changes, hardly the dry, single-minded approach assumed by economic theory.

## Mood

It is no secret to anyone that mood affects behavior, and there is no logical reason why financial behavior would be an exception. While investor mood is very difficult to quantify, isolate, or research under controlled conditions, it would be difficult to dismiss the likelihood that it impacts the stock market. Mood is also fleeting and is likely to be intertwined with other effects, making it even more challenging to understand. We can see, however, from extreme examples such as the events of September 11, 2001, that mood can have a dramatic impact on the markets. Few analysts would deny that the depth of the market's negative reaction to 9/11 was caused by a massive mood shift, since the true economic impact of that day's events couldn't even be fully assessed at first. Whether you characterize that mood shift as anger, grief, pessimism, shock, or a combination of all these emotions, it was very clear in its net effect on the market. Similarly, the mood shifted quickly back to one of confidence, resolve, and patriotism within a matter of days, taking the market just as quickly in the other direction.

One area of research that demonstrates how mood shifts affect the markets is the sports effect. In a 2007 article in the *Journal of Finance*, Professors Edmans, Garcia, and Norli cited the results of studies that show losses in major sports events lead to a negative effect on stock market prices immediately after. In their words,

> Motivated by psychological evidence of a strong link between soccer outcomes and mood, we use international soccer results as our primary mood variable. Using a cross-section of 39 countries, we find that losses in soccer matches have an economically and statistically significant negative effect on the losing country's stock market. For example, elimination from a major international soccer tournament is associated with a next-day return on the national stock market index that is 38 basis points lower than average. . . . A loss in the World Cup elimination stage leads to a next-day abnormal stock return of –49 basis points. . . . We also document a loss effect after international cricket, rugby, and basketball games. . . . Overall, our interpretation of the evidence is that the loss effect is caused by a change in investor mood.[14]

Believe it or not, the *sunshine effect* is another example of how mood affects markets, and its magnitude is surprisingly substantial. Skeptics may roll their eyes, but there is much evidence in support of this effect. One academic study by David Hirshleifer and Tyler Shumway examined the relation between morning sunshine at a country's leading stock exchange and market index stock returns that day at twenty-six stock exchanges around the world from 1982 to 1997. The researchers concluded, "Sunshine is strongly significantly correlated with daily stock returns. After controlling for sunshine, rain and snow are unrelated to returns. . . . These findings are difficult to reconcile with fully rational price-setting."[15] The researches also concluded that in New York City, the annualized nominal market return on perfectly sunny days is approximately 24.8 percent per year versus 8.7 percent per year on perfectly cloudy days.

Investor sentiment, such as that measured by the University of Michigan's polls, is somewhat of a public mood analyzer at least as it applies to optimism or pessimism regarding the economy. But mood can be interpreted much more broadly to include emotions ranging from fear to euphoria. With regard to sentiment, Baker and Wurgler demonstrated that "when beginning-of-period proxies for sentiment are low, subsequent returns are relatively high for small stocks, young stocks, high volatility stocks, unprofitable stocks, non-dividend-paying stocks, extreme growth stocks, and distressed stocks. When sentiment is high, on the other hand, these categories of stock earn relatively low subsequent returns."[16] In other words, buying when sentiment is high (positive) means you are paying something of a sentiment premium and are likely to get lower returns than if you buy when sentiment is low. Using this line of thought, contrarians view mood extremes (as measured by consumer sentiment figures) to represent a contrary indicator of market tops and bottoms, and the evidence bears this out at the extremes. However, the market's condition (whether strong or weak at the time) is itself a determinant of mood, so sentiment extremes are usually used to confirm or deny market bottoms rather than predict them.

Overconfidence is a widespread and persistent human trait, and its prevalence is well documented. People are notoriously overconfident about themselves, their abilities, their marriages, their business skills, and many other things. "Psychologists have determined that overconfidence causes people to overestimate their knowledge, underestimate risks, and exaggerate their ability to control events. Security selection . . . is precisely the type of task at which people exhibit the greatest overconfidence."[17]

Overconfidence manifests itself in a number of different ways in stock investing. Among others:

1. Investors misjudge the true odds of success in trading situations.
2. Investors unrealistically believe they have information or insights others don't have.
3. Those who experience short-term investing success tend to view that success as the result of their own trading skills rather than to random chance, which is most often the case.
4. People trade their individual accounts more frequently than they should to optimize their success, and thereby reduce their returns accordingly.

On this last point, Barber and Odean analyzed the trading activities of 10,000 individual investors with discount brokerage accounts, as cited previously in Chapter 5.[18] They found that, on average, the more people traded, the worse they did. In addition, men traded more and did worse than women investors. The results showed that trading more actively resulted in lower returns by individuals and that the stocks they sell outperform the ones they buy. In an efficient market, uninformed investors should earn a prevailing return similar to that of the overall market. Naturally, higher transaction volume generates higher transaction costs, which will have the effect of reducing investor returns. But the investors in Odean's study performed worse than the market, even after adjusting for the higher transaction costs. This implies that small investors, as a group, systematically sell winners too soon as well as potentially pick stocks too early.

Yale professor Robert Shiller has written,

> Another aspect of overconfidence is that people tend to make judg-
> ments in uncertain situations by looking for familiar patterns and
> assuming that future patterns will resemble past ones, often with-
> out sufficient consideration of the reasons for the pattern or the
> probability of the pattern repeating itself. This anomaly of human
> judgment . . . was demonstrated in a number of experiments by
> psychologists Tversky and Kahneman.[19]

## QUASI-MAGICAL THINKING

Another of Robert Shiller's papers describes a tendency by people
to act as if their actions have unnatural powers: "The term quasi-
magical thinking, as defined by Shafir and Tversky (1992), is used to
describe situations in which people act as if they erroneously believe
that their actions can influence an outcome (as with magical thinking) but in which they in fact do not believe this. It includes acting
as if one thinks that one can take actions that will, in effect, undo
what is obviously predetermined, or that one can change history."[20]
With stocks, people have actually exhibited the notion that their
loyalty to a stock that has declined in value (whether through purchase or holding) will help it come back in price. It is probably not
too dissimilar from the notion that rooting for your favorite sports
team helps it win more.

## REPRESENTATIVENESS

Evidenced once again in studies by Kahneman and Tversky, there is
a tendency by individuals to assume a small sample of data as typical
or representative of a broader conclusion than the laws of probability would suggest. In the financial world, *representativeness* can lead
to faulty assumptions and several biases, including *base rate neglect*
and *sample-size neglect*. In statistical terms, that means they apply
Bayes's law incorrectly. In layman's terms, it means people jump to
often-biased conclusions from small data sets that are not necessarily representative of the larger data population. This also means
that people often believe that they see patterns in what are actually
random sequences.

Another form of representativeness is noted by Shefrin, who defines it as "judgments based on stereotypes." He notes

> De Bondt and Thaler find that stocks that have been extreme past losers in the preceding three years, do much better than extreme past winners over the subsequent three years. De Bondt (1992) shows that the long-term earnings forecasts made by security analysts tend to be biased in the direction of recent success. Specifically, analysts overreact in that they are much more optimistic about recent winners than they are about recent losers.[21]

### Other Behavioral Themes

The behavioral effects noted earlier have been studied and made public by noted academic professionals, but practitioners in the securities industry have observed even more. From the thousands of individual investors I have observed over the span of my career, I have coined a few of my own biases.

*Stock revenge* is the notion that traders or company insiders are presumed to act in such a manner as to make a stock go their way instead of yours (typically down after you've bought it); by not selling, you are going to "get them back."

With a *jinx*, an investor is caught in a catch-22 in which the very action of buying a stock imbues it with bad luck and makes it go down.

*George's heuristic* describes a common behavior that prevents people from taking a profit while a stock is rising. It is similar to the mental anguish people exhibit when they are determined to buy and hold a portfolio of stocks for years and years. Despite his more than 30 years as an investment professional, my good friend George still carries around much of the same human psychological baggage exhibited by nonprofessional investors. He knows it, and he acknowledges that his mentality will never change. (It's knowing people like George that convinces me almost nobody is capable of removing themselves from the psychological legacy of our human forefathers.) George likes to find undervalued stocks that are "breaking out" in price and ride them higher. George's heuristic kicks in once he's purchased. He sets vague mental price targets but rarely holds to them. As long as the stock is rising, he holds on, frequently buying more on the way up. Rare, of course, is the stock that continues to go straight up. When a material correction sets in, George will agonize, convincing himself that it will eventually begin rising again. He holds until the pain of loss forces him to sell, all but ensuring that he will always sell on the way down, rather than up.

With *itchy money*, many people, and a huge preponderance of financial professionals, suffer from the obsession of having to put their money somewhere in stocks at all times.

The *fear of being left out* is probably a subset of herding. This syndrome is evident in people who exhibit a notable tendency to be perturbed when others around them are making money and they are not. This is readily seen in fad stocks and market bubbles where people are willing to pay extraordinary prices just to get in the game and not be left out. This may be a similar effect to the "keep up with the Joneses" phenomenon we used to hear about in the context of conspicuous consumption.

And my personal favorite . . .

*Conspiracy* is the notion that colluding groups of investment houses, hedge funds, high-powered and wealthy individuals, and the U.S. government conspire to move the market where it will most benefit them, whether it makes sense to us or not. One variation on the conspiracy theme holds that the U.S. government finances a stealth organization referred to as the *plunge protection team* (PPT). The PPT is supposedly the white knight that comes in and buys stocks (or derivatives) to save us when it appears that the market is ready to fall off a cliff. This notion is derived from a group by that name that was actually formed after the crash of 1987 by Ronald Reagan. As established by Executive Order 12631, the working group consists of the Treasury secretary, the chair of the board of governors of the Federal Reserve System, the chair of the Securities and Exchange Commission, and the chair of the Commodity Futures Trading Commission. The group's mission is to prevent such calamities in the future.

## CONCLUSIONS

These pages hardly do justice to the more than thirty years of published literature in the field of financial psychology, behavioral finance, or any other name by which it's known. Researchers have only scratched the surface of this vast and complex subject and will no doubt conduct countless more studies in years to come. What we are certain of at this point is that there are lots of characteristically human ways in which we exercise judgments, consider alternatives, make decisions, and take actions with regard to investing, and that they do not necessarily fit the assumptions of rational investing in classic economic theory. But we have only reached the first level of identifying these effects' characteristics and understanding how they each affect us. We do not yet have even the slightest appreciation of how these characteristics interact with each other, change over time or with circumstances, are affected by exogenous forces or events, or affect the market's behavior. As such, the implementation of behavioral finance to develop investment strategy occurs at no more than a handful of organizations today and only as an adjunct to the traditional approach.

Am I suggesting that we should replace ourselves as managers of our (or other people's) investments with a computer that won't be subject to our human failings? Should we be gearing our investment strategy to the weather reports in New York? Or should we just accept our humble position in the human herd and buy an index fund to hold forever? I am suggesting none of these, but while the research continues to isolate these heuristics and biases, we can utilize this information now in the formulation and execution of investment strategy. Over time, we may know much more about the complexities of human behavior as it applies to financial markets. But if history is any indication, then that could easily be another twenty, thirty, or fifty years or more at the rate things are progressing in that field. Meanwhile, it behooves us to take our heads out of the sand, acknowledge that there *is* an impact, and concede that it may be substantial. In Part III of this book, I will offer a method of visually analyzing the market and interpreting the tone and direction of the herd's actions.

## Chapter Notes

1. William F. Sharpe, *Investors and Markets: Portfolio Choices, Asset Prices, and Investment Advice* (Princeton, NJ: Princeton University Press, 2007), p. 10.
2. Dan Ariely, *Predictably Irrational* (New York: HarperCollins, 2008), p. xx.

3. Andrei Shleifer, *Inefficient Markets* (New York: Oxford University Press, 2000), p. 10.
4. Daniel Kahneman and Amos Tversky, *Choices, Values, and Frames* (New York: Cambridge University Press, 2000), p. 17.
5. Richard L. Peterson, *Inside the Investor's Brain* (New York: John Wiley & Sons, 2007), p. 38.
6. Paul Slovic, Melissa Finucane, Ellen Peters, and Donald G. MacGregor, "The Affect Heuristic" in Thomas Gilovich, Dale Griffin, and Daniel Kahneman (Eds.), *Heuristics and Biases* (New York: Cambridge University Press, 2009), p. 419.
7. Ariely, *Predictably Irrational*, p. 239.
8. Jack L. Knetsch, "The Endowment Effect and Evidence of Nonreversible Indifference Curves," *American Economic Review*, 79(5) (December 1989): p. 1277.
9. Kahneman and Tversky, *Choices, Values, and Frames*, p. 220.
10. Ibid., p. 210.
11. Nassim Nicholas Taleb, *The Black Swan* (New York: Random House, 2007), p. 150.
12. Terry Burnham, *Mean Markets and Lizard Brains* (New York: John Wiley & Sons, 2005), p. 30.
13. Hirsch Shefrin, *Beyond Greed and Fear* (New York: Oxford University Press, 2002), p. 126.
14. Alex Edmans, Diego Garcia, and Øyvind Norli, "Sports Sentiment and Stock Returns," *Journal of Finance*, 62(4) (August 2007): 1967-1998.
15. David Hirshleifer and Tyler Shumway, "Good Day Sunshine: Stock Returns and the Weather," *Journal of Finance*, 58(3) (June 2003): p. 1011.
16. Malcolm Baker and Jeffrey Wurgler, "Investor Sentiment and the Cross-Section of Stock Returns," *Journal of Finance*, 61(4): pp. 1645-1680.
17. David Hirshleifer, "Investor Psychology and Asset Pricing," *Journal of Finance*, 56(4) (August 2001): p. 1540, 1542.
18. Brad Barber and Terrance Odean, "The Common Stock Investment Performance of Individual Investors," *Journal of Finance*, Vol. LV, No. 2, April 2000, pp. 773-806.
19. Robert J. Shiller, *Irrational Exuberance* (New York: Doubleday, 2005), p. 153.
20. Robert Shiller, "Human Behavior and the Efficiency of the Financial System," in John B. Taylor and Michael Woodford (Eds.), *Handbook of Macroeconomics* (Amsterdam: Elsevier), Vol 1, 1999, pp. 1305-1340.
21. Shefrin, *Beyond Greed and Fear*, p. 16.

# Anomalies 8

*Random walkers eat your heart out![1]*

YALE HIRSCH, *Stock Trader's Almanac*

**anom·aly:** A deviation from the norm or from a common rule; an incongruity, irregularity, or inconsistency.

Y EARS AGO, stock market anomalies may have been little more than interesting factoids to throw out at cocktail parties. But these days their existence takes on new meaning as evidence of the way human behavior manifests itself in market behavior.

To identify a stock market anomaly using the definition above, one must first determine what is "normal" or what "common rules" are applicable. If one believes that the behavior of stocks is described by a random walk, then one could justify an extremely wide variation in market behavior as being within normal bounds. Behavioral experts Daniel Kahneman and Amos Tversky describe market anomalies as follows: "Economics can be distinguished from other social sciences by the belief that most (all?) behavior can be explained by assuming that agents have stable, well-defined preferences and make rational choices consistent with those preferences. . . . An empirical result qualifies as an anomaly if it is difficult to 'rationalize,' or if implausible assumptions are necessary to explain it within the paradigm."[2] The paradigm is the efficient market.

Let's look at real situations rather than argue semantics. Most of us would view a three-legged frog as an anomaly but would we have the same regard for General Motors stock at $5 per share when it has been trading between \$20 and \$75 over the last ten years? No, because although an abnormally high or low stock price relative to an historic trading range may represent a perceived trading opportunity, that's not what constitutes a market anomaly. The common interpretation of stock market anomalies focuses on recurring, systematic situations in the pricing of a certain type, sector, or group of securities that does not conform to the expected (i.e., normal) behavior of an efficient market. In essence, a market anomaly can be anything from a simple mispricing opportunity, such as an acquisition target that does not reflect the announced value of the purchase even after normal discounting, to a characteristic of the overall market, such as the legendary Christmas rally (an annual run up between Christmas and New Year's Eve).

Anomalies, whether based on behavior or due to other inherent factors that exist in the market, represent cracks in the random walk. By accepting that human behavior shapes the market and that anomalies exist, we place ourselves in a position to accept that the market's movements may not only be partially explainable but also predictable.

Proponents of the efficient markets theory hold that a certain degree of irrational trading always exists, creating mispricings that are temporary and quickly corrected by the forces of arbitrage or informed market traders. Malkiel maintains that market anomalies, even if definitively identified, are unlikely to be dependable in the long run, unlikely to be significant enough to overcome the added burden of taxes and transaction costs, and unlikely to remain in existence very long, once made known to the public. But, substantial evidence to the contrary has been presented. There are anomalies that persist.

Chapter 7 explored human behavior as it applies to investing and determined that behavioral information is used in two ways: (1) to examine the way it affects individuals when they trade or invest and (2) to determine how the common behavioral characteristics of large numbers of investors causes a definable pattern of behavior in the market as a whole. This chapter will look in the reverse direction and identify observed market anomalies, regardless of whether there is a directly attributable behavior causing them. Market anomalies existed long before behavioral finance was ever defined.

## ARBITRAGE

The quintessential stock market anomaly is the arbitrage opportunity—that fleeting, often miniscule mispricing of a security that can be exploited with little or no risk. From an arbitrage perspective, a mispriced security has nothing to do with fundamentals or intrinsic value. It is the pricing relationship between two or more securities, or between securities and their derivatives, that arbitrageurs generally feed on since their preference is to effect strategies that hold little or no risk. Buying or selling a security simply because it is perceived to be under- or overvalued doesn't entice the professional arbitrageur because it entails risk. Pure arbitrage, when executed properly, is essentially riskless. The creation, for example, of a *conversion* trade whereby the arbitrageur purchases a stock, purchases a put option on that stock, and sells a call option at the same month and strike price locks in a riskless profit potential that is realized when the options expire.

There are also *risk arbitrage* strategies that aren't quite riskless but still represent a high-odds gamble. Dividend arbitrage and merger arbitrage would fall into this category. In an announced merger for stock (rather than a cash acquisition), traders will short an acquiring company's stock and purchase the stock of the target, provided of course that the deal price and the time to consummation provide a healthy premium over the risk-free interest rate. (The risk comes in when a deal actually changes or falls through.) Dividend arbitrage on liquid, high-dividend stocks like R.J. Reynolds can frequently account for hundreds of thousands of shares and their attendant call options changing hands prior to the issuance of a dividend.

Perhaps the granddaddy of arbitrage from a capital-allocation standpoint is index futures arbitrage. When the Standard & Poor's (S&P) futures sufficiently diverge in price from the index itself (as happens frequently), arbitrageurs can either buy or sell them and subsequently execute a *program trade* (a one-button transaction that buys or sells a multitude of preselected stocks simultaneously) to capitalize on the price differential. If interest rates are 3 percent annually for short-term money and a position needs to be held for one month until futures expiration, then the arbitrage trade needs only to make 1/12 of 3 percent, or about 0.25 percent, to cover the interest and be profitable. In an era of exceedingly low interest rates and high volatility, this type of arbitrage occurs in huge numbers.

The common theme to all these forms of arbitrage is that they revolve around price discrepancies and are essentially riskless. The big brokerages all have traders armed to the teeth with sophisticated computers that are trained not just to zero in on arbitrage opportunities as they arise in daily trading, but to execute complex inter-market trades with a single push of a button. Thus, it is widely acknowledged that individuals cannot realistically expect to compete against the pros for riskless arbitrage opportunities. Professionals have ways to make easy and substantially risk-free profits that are simply unavailable to the general public; it's a fact of life and is viewed as a plus for the efficient functioning of the markets. Random and efficient market fans argue that the small discrepancies that arbitrageurs thrive on are miniscule and, for all intents and purposes, irrelevant to the action of the overall market.

The anomalies discussed here are those that are not considered arbitrage—in other words, the persistent ones that cannot be arbitraged away without risk. Those who hunt for anomalies tend to be more concerned with the resulting market action than with the cause, though having at least some idea of the cause increases confidence in the ability to exploit the effect. Some anomalies can be traced to specific behavioral phenomena. Others, however, may be little more than empirical observations that cannot easily be tied to a single root cause or that may represent the combined result of multiple causes interacting in dynamic ways too complex to fully understand.

The inability to assign many market anomalies a root cause invites proponents of the random market to discredit them. They argue that once made public, anomalies of any consequence will be acted on or anticipated by enough market participants to effectively dissolve them. Nonetheless, there is ample evidence of anomalies that do persist, and Dr. Vijay Singal, author of *Beyond the Random Walk*, responds thusly to this argument: "Though anomalies should disappear in an efficient market, they may persist because they are not well understood, arbitrage is too costly, the profit potential is insufficient, trading restrictions exist, and behavioral biases exist."[3] Anomalies are indeed subject to changing causal factors and mitigation from informed traders. Therefore, anomaly hunters need to be attentive to changes in the nature and magnitude of anomalies over time. In addition, just as the anomalies represent statistical aberrations from what would be expected in a perfectly efficient market, the anomalies themselves are based on statistical evidence that might have been derived from hundreds or thousands of data points. As such, they too are subject to variation and may result in a reduced or enhanced version of what was expected.

Singal notes that, "academics and practitioners have expended tens of thousands of man-years researching mispricings and anomalies."[4] By and large, however, Singal acknowledges that most of this published material has been confined to academic journals. These anomalies and inefficiencies identify specific instances in which the random walk thesis doesn't hold; such instances are seen as opportunities that may potentially be exploited for profit or at least worthy of consideration when implementing one's investment strategy. Some of these anomalies are relatively easy to build into an existing strategy, while others would require constructing a specific strategy around them, and still others are too isolated and impractical for individual investors to exploit at all.

### INHERENT FACTORS

In Chapter 8, I examined investor behavior as a homogenous group, focusing on the common psychological traits we share as human beings. From another perspective, our roles in the market are actually quite different depending on what constituency we represent: professional traders, individual investors, brokers, portfolio managers, market makers, institutions, arbitrageurs, fund managers, specialists, and so on. Each has its own behavioral characteristics that stem from the role it plays in the markets, and what is rational for one might well be irrational for another. Each has a somewhat unique set of constraints, parameters, incentives, risk tolerance, tax profile, and competitive environment. The differences in the rules and roles of these various groups also impact how the overall market behaves, and I refer to them as *inherent factors.* If you are looking to develop a more effective approach to stock investing through a better understanding of what makes the market move, then understanding the effect of behavioral factors such as those discussed in the previous chapter is certainly key. But they don't explain the whole picture any more than fundamental analysis does. The market's overall behavior is a complex, interdependent function of underlying economic fundamentals, behavioral characteristics of the participants, and the inherent characteristics of market constituents.

Harvard economics professor Andrei Shleifer has written about institutions and what he calls "additional distortions caused by their role in the markets."[5] Shleifer's point is valid: institutional volume dwarfs that of individual investors, who now represent only a small portion of direct trading volume (estimated at maybe 20 percent). The inherent characteristics of trading institutions have an effect on market behavior. Mutual funds, for example, are bound by rules that require them to remain fully invested (except to maintain as much as 5 percent cash for liquidity considerations), and they must honor requests for new shares or redemptions from investors on the day of request. That means that when investors request redemptions on equity funds, even if only to switch to bond or money market funds within the same fund family, the funds must immediately (the same day) liquidate sufficient amounts of equities to meet those redemptions, regardless of whether the portfolio managers believe it is a good time to sell. During wild swings, and particularly during moments of fear or panic on the part of individuals, the rush to the door forces mutual funds to either purchase or liquidate huge amounts of stocks in hurried fashion, often causing an exacerbated movement in the markets. Were there no mutual funds, the actions by individuals to liquidate stocks would likely be spread out over a longer time frame and have a lower effect on overall volatility.

This effect has been made even more acute by the tremendous shift in retirement assets over the last twenty years from corporate pension plans—where the assets were managed as a single pool by the employer—to 401(k) plans that are directed by individual participants who are generally able to effect same-day transactions through online accounts. Whether it is a 401(k), an individual retirement account, or a regular investment account, individuals are now widely able to access their accounts online and cause a mutual fund company to undergo forced liquidation (or purchase) of an entire portfolio of stocks. This was clearly evident during mid-October 2008 when markets were selling off and huge fund liquidations were causing final hour declines on the Dow Jones Industrial Averages of several hundred points or more after hundreds of points of declines during earlier trading hours.

Margin selling is another type of forced liquidation that occurs at the individual level. Margin liquidations are imposed on us by regulation and, by nature, occur most often when our portfolios are losing value—a time when it may not otherwise be advantageous to sell. In market declines, margin selling occurs in a systematic fashion and is neither random nor a behavioral quirk. Forced liquidations occur at institutions as well. The forced liquidations at hedge funds that were highly leveraged were found to be responsible for a great deal of selling in both stocks and commodities during the fall of 2008.

Numerous other inherent factors are known to exist and to affect market behavior:

- Institutional window dressing occurs at the end of each month and quarter as portfolio managers add or subtract specific items from portfolios that will appear more gratifying to the audience who will be reading the portfolio's quarter-end or month-end statements.
- Benchmarking to an index is an almost universal activity for portfolio managers. Accordingly, they design and execute portfolios specifically related to the benchmarks they are measured against. Managers also benchmark to one another for peer comparisons. This also creates price movements not totally consistent with random markets.

- Index changes also cause aberrations that are not the result of enhanced buy interest due to fundamentals but of artificial buy interest on the part of index funds that must sell the security being jettisoned by the index and buy the one replacing it.
- Though mentioned in Chapter 7 as a form of herding, the sales activity of brokers may also be viewed as an inherent factor in that they continuously advocate buying stocks, regardless of market valuations, economic cycles, or any other reason why not buying might be in the client's better interest. As long as there are brokers, this activity will prevail, as it is in the interest of their livelihood to do so.

It is not my intent to explore these factors in detail for purposes of this book. Even if one could identify all of the major factors, quantifying them is almost impossible, particularly in isolation. The point is that these and other inherent factors cause action by market participants that is not consistent with an ideally efficient market scenario and that may lead to exploitable opportunities or to enhanced decision making within the context of existing strategies. I bring them up to support my contention that a substantial number of such factors exist and that they may be important not just individually but also in aggregate.

### The Wisdom of Yale

A number of anomalies are tied to the calendar and have been publicly chronicled by Yale Hirsch ever since he began publishing his classic *Stock Trader's Almanac* in 1966. The almanac is chock-full of statistical market data that the Hirsh family has dutifully documented every year since. Despite his name, Yale was not a professor and did not publish his findings in academic journals. Nevertheless, Yale Hirsch made one of the largest practical contributions to the field of behavioral finance, and he did so long before much of the behavioral research had even been published.

Unlike papers published in academic journals, Hirsch's publication contains no complicated theoretical justifications, no references to dozens of other related papers, and no complex mathematical theories—just straightforward, empirical observations you can use or not use at your discretion. Nonetheless, the Hirsches have uncovered important evidence as to the nonrandom nature of the stock market. While people could read interesting ditties from Hirsch about the days before major holidays or performance during election years, also included were some extremely significant market anomalies such as the famous *January effect* and the *best six months* discovery.

## THE JANUARY EFFECT

One of the most widely publicized market anomalies, the so-called January effect, is often misinterpreted to imply that stocks rise in January. Though history since 1950 does give the month of January about two-thirds likelihood of being a positive month, the expected return in statistical terms for an index like the S&P 500 Index would only be about 0.85 percent for the month on average. Furthermore, the variation from year to year (as low as –7.1 percent in 1960 and as high as 13.2 percent in 1987) would not present a compelling enough case by itself to warrant much special attention. The January effect is really about how small cap stocks outperform large caps, and it actually begins in December. Hirsch noted that between 1953 and 1995, the S&P low-priced index outperformed the S&P 500 during the month of January forty out of forty-three times and by a fourfold average![6] The effect drew much attention and became quite well known over the years, yet continued to persist even though everyone seemed to know it was coming. Hirsch later revised his analysis by switching to the Russell 1000 and Russell 2000 indexes for his comparison. The data shows considerable outperformance by the small caps, with the most pronounced advantage coming during the last two weeks of December and then tailing off (though still advantageous) all the way through February. The most plausible explanation for this phenomenon centers on tax-related selling in December followed by purchases in January and February. However, tax selling alone doesn't comfortably explain the entire effect, since there is a similar but short-lived effect prior to Labor Day, when tax selling should have almost nothing to do with it.

Vijay Singal goes even deeper into the January anomaly by dividing stocks into groups by market capitalization and by their respective price rise or decline during the prior year. By doing this, Singal focuses his research on those companies that are both the smallest and have declined the most in value compared with those that are both the largest companies and have appreciated the most. He concludes that the January effect is even more pronounced between these "small losers" and "large gainers." He finds that the small losers tend to lose value in December and then gain mightily in January, while the large losers gain in both November and December and then barely rise at all in January. This can be refined even further by looking at the last five days in December plus the first five days in January as the most dramatic part of the period. In this manner, Singal's data produces dramatic results that show the small losers gaining between 2.8 percent and 29 percent for that 10-day period since 1988 through 2000 and never having a decline. (The Tax Reform Act of 1986 moved the end of the tax year for mutual funds to October from December and would have affected the data prior to that period.) On the other hand, the large winners showed negative returns for all but one year, with a range of +.34 percent to –10 percent.[7] Clearly, a strategy of shorting large winners and purchasing small losers could potentially produce an exceptional return during this period and would be somewhat immune to the overall market direction during the period. As long as tax selling remains a reality for individual investors and as long as the anomaly is misunderstood or misplayed, it is likely to remain in effect.

### Best Six Months

The best six months phenomenon is even more straightforward. It refers to the fact that over the last half of the twentieth century (1950–2000), the six-month period of November 1 through April 30 outperformed the alternate six-month period from May 1 through October 31 by such an overwhelming margin that the November period accounted for 99.6 percent of the total gain over fifty years while the May period accounted for the other 0.4 percent. Put another way, "$10,000 invested during the best six months (November through April) gained the investor $363,367, but if you were to invest the same amount in the other six months of the year, the gain would have just been $11,582."[8]

The best six months phenomenon lends credence to the old Wall Street adage, "Sell in May and go away." The cause of this anomaly is not as clear as the January effect and is likely to involve a far more complex rationale relating to multiple factors. One might assume a contributing factor to be the higher likelihood of people acquiring additional money from holiday or year-end bonuses followed by tax refunds while being relieved of money in summer and fall as a result of vacation and school expenses. This logic is somewhat supported by the fact that in the early twentieth century, farming was the occupation of as much as a third of all Americans and August (harvest month for many) was the best performing month of the year for the stock market. Since the middle of the century, the reduction in personal farming has resulted in August now being one of the worst performing months.

In direct opposition to efficient market rationale, it is easy to see how an anomaly such as the best six months can persist despite its magnitude and the ease of implementation. The idea of buying and holding is by far the prevalent modus operandi for stock investing in this country. Individuals see and hear stories about Christmas rallies or summer rallies, but they rarely take these rallies seriously as an investment strategy. If they are in for the long haul, then the idea of being out of equities entirely for six months of the year would be perceived as ludicrous—despite the above evidence. Then, of course, there would be the tax and transaction charge consequences. In addition, if there are brokers or portfolio managers involved, there would be huge opposition from them, as that would undermine their supposed talents as financial experts. No portfolio manager can justify being out of the market for six months while still collecting fees from the client for managing the money, and few would take the chance of going against the herd based on a statistic that no one could explain and that has no economic justification. Managers rarely even consider the effects of bona fide economic or business cycle data, much less something as unrelated as the calendar—heaven forbid! No manager would want to defend the practice in an arbitration hearing when the client missed a small rally in September. Given the overriding mentality about investing in this country, this one will likely persist for some time.

### SEASONAL EFFECTS

Josef Lakonishok (University of Illinois) and Seymour Smidt (Cornell University) examined ninety years of data on seasonal anomalies and concluded the following:

> DJIA returns are persistently anomalous over a ninety-year period around the turn of the week, around the turn of the month, around the turn of the year, and around holidays. Specifically, the rate of return on Mondays is substantially negative (–0.14 percent), the price increase around the turn of the month exceeds the total monthly price increase, the price increase from the last trading day before Christmas to the end of the year is over 1.5 percent, and the rate of return before holidays is more than twenty times the normal rate of return. The possibility that these particular anomalies could have occurred by chance cannot be excluded, but this is very unlikely.[9]

## OTHER ANOMALIES

Though there are many correlated patterns in market movement and chronological events, anomalies are not tied exclusively to the calendar. In many cases, they appear in other unusual places. Below are a few of the most pervasive.

### SHORT-TERM PRICE DRIFT

Contrary to the efficient market hypothesis notion that information gets fully priced into a stock almost immediately on public dissemination, research shows pronounced and persistent "price drift" for many days following major announcements, whether in a positive or a negative direction. The data suggests that price drift is not discernible in all situations but is particularly evident when there is a public announcement by the company and an attendant rise in trading volume. According to Singal, "Indeed, if large price changes are accompanied by an increase in volume and a public announcement by management or analysts, then a price continuation is likely to result in a one-month abnormal return of about 3.5 percent for positive events and –2.25 percent for negative events."[10] Defining "abnormal return" as the incremental return over the S&P 500, Singal calculates that even after transaction costs, this anomaly could represent a potential increment over the S&P benchmark of 15 percent to 36 percent on an annualized basis.

### REPORTED INSIDER TRADING ACTIVITY

Though more difficult both to analyze and act on, reported data on insider activity has also been shown to produce materially anomalous results when used as an indicator of the likelihood of a stock rising or falling. Singal used the insider activity as reported by the *Wall Street Journal* in December 2001, implementing either buys or sells beginning in January 2002 and running through the following June. His resulting test sample, adjusted for several criteria including insider trades deemed to be associated with option exercises, resulted in the returns indicated in **TABLE 8.1**.

While impressive, these results may even understate the anomalous effect of insider buys and sells. After this test was completed, the reporting rules for insider trades were changed from the tenth day of the following month (which could delay public notice for as

Table 8-1    Trades Based on Reported Insider Activity

|  | Number of Positions | Period Return (%) | S&P 500 Period Return (%) | Incremental Gain or Loss (%) | Gain or Loss Annualized (%) |
|---|---|---|---|---|---|
| Sells | 15 | –28.6 | –13.8 | 14.8 | 29.6 |
| Buys | 26 | + 15 | –13.8 | 28.8 | 56.7 |

Source: Vijay Singal from *Beyond the Random Walk*

many as 40 days after the trade occurred) to just two business days. This much shorter requirement should have the effect of revealing insider activity sooner, thereby enhancing the effect of this anomaly in the marketplace.

The reasons why insider activity should represent a valid predictor of company strength or weakness are intuitive—company executives and directors are better informed than the general public about the status and prospects of their businesses. The reasons why the anomaly persists may be less obvious. Though publicly available, interpreting insider activity can be seriously misleading unless adjustments are made for the fact that insiders sell a multiple of how much they buy due to stock-option exercises. Exercises result in sales for which there is no attending purchase offset in the public market, and they tend to represent the realization of a benefit rather than an action taken in anticipation of a company's prospects. Furthermore, there is no way to tell how much of sales due to option exercise represent anticipation of a decline in stock price versus the fact that the options are expiring.

### The IPO Anomaly

A variety of factors particular to initial public offerings (IPOs) help demonstrate how extreme in magnitude an anomaly can be over what an efficient market would expect. Investment banks routinely underprice IPOs to ensure that they sell out and then grow rapidly afterward. This not only reduces their risk of having to "eat" any unsold shares on the offering but also ensures that happy customers will keep coming back for more. In a dramatic statement of just how much IPOs are artificially underpriced, G. William Schwert at University of Rochester points out that $1,000 invested in a portfolio of IPOs compounded since 1960 (buying the IPO, selling a month later, and buying a new IPO) would have generated a portfolio by 2001 of $533 \times 10^{33}$ (that's 33 zeroes!) compared with $74,000 in the Center for Research in Security Prices portfolio (value-weighted market portfolio of the New York Stock Exchange, or NYSE). It seems as if the investment banks have their own special way of keeping the things efficient!

## THE PRESIDENTIAL ANOMALY

With another somewhat compelling and intuitive anomaly cited by Yale and Jeffrey Hirsch, the last two years (pre-election year and election year) of a presidential cycle outperforming the first two years by more than 3:1 (745.9 percent versus 227.6 percent) between 1833 and 2004. By themselves, the final years in the cycle (pre-election years) outperformed election years, postelection years, and midterm years by ratios of almost 2:1, 3:1, and 7:1 respectively. Hirsch rationalizes the numbers this way: "In an effort to gain reelection, presidents tend to take care of most of their more painful initiatives in the first half of their term and 'prime the pump' in the second half so the electorate is most prosperous when they enter the voting booths."[11]

## OTHER NOTABLE ANOMALIES

The following additional anomalies are worthy of mention:

- In 1981, Banz and Reinganum demonstrated that small cap NYSE firms yielded higher average returns than Sharpe and Lintner's famous capital asset-pricing model suggested.
- In 1980, Ken French noted that returns over the weekends were systematically and reliably negative during the period from 1953 to 1977. Kamstra, Kramer, and Levi (2000) further discovered that on the specific weekends where daylight saving goes into effect or returns to normal time, large negative returns on financial market indexes follow (roughly 200 to 500 percent of the regular weekend effect), and they argue that the effect could be a direct result of changes in sleep patterns.[12] (Schwert concluded that both the size and weekend anomalies appeared to have been eliminated or attenuated in more recent years.[13])
- Open-end funds appear to demonstrate a *cold hands effect* in which poorly performing managers tend to continue underperforming for years rather than revert to a mean level of performance by occasionally outperforming, as statistics would predict.

## CONCLUSIONS

A number of books and perhaps hundreds of academic papers have been written on market anomalies—so many, in fact, that criticisms have even been launched from within academia itself over the possible tendency to mine the data in search of anything that might qualify as a market anomaly (the idea being that if you look hard enough you can find just about anything you want in a large enough data universe). Nevertheless, the sheer volume of such research, most of which is supported by known or intuitively accepted causal factors, leads us to the conclusion that anomalies do exist and can be fleeting or persist for some time, if not indefinitely. By their existence, anomalies thus provide proof that the market has many nonrandom traits after all. The identification of these anomalies demonstrates not just that there are ways to enhance returns by investing at certain times of year but also that the overall behavior of the market is riddled with ways in which market efficiency is superseded by human behavior or other inherent factors.

Anomalies can be challenging to isolate and to research with high degrees of confidence. Tests for anomalies tend to cover wide swaths of time such as at least twenty years and generally more than fifty years in order to be considered statistically valid. But with numerous inherent market factors existing only for the last ten to twenty years and psychological factors changing all the time, research for those extended periods of time may actually be providing misleading results by spanning periods in which certain contributing factors may not even have existed. In addition, anomalies change over time both in nature and magnitude, and their effect must be assumed to be either mitigated or enhanced by other anomalies or spurious market factors. This may keep the academics busy for some time to come, but for practical purposes it makes life difficult for those seeking to exploit such phenomena. As such, I am not recommending any of those discussed in this chapter for individual exploitation. Should you be interested in doing that, I recommend reading more detail about the nature of these anomalies from the sources referenced in the endnotes.

My interest in market anomalies is how, in aggregate, they become part of the fabric of the overall market and contribute to its behavior. If there were a way to read or interpret that overall behavior, even in a small way, then there might be a way to profit from market moves other than the multiyear average rise expected from the standard buy-and-hold approach. From Chapter 5, we know the market moves many, many multiples of the long-term growth rate each year. In the fall of 2008, the market frequently moved 5 percent to 10 percent in a single day yet many investors sat idly by, praying that when all is said and done, they would not only have their principal intact but also realize a modest return of 10 percent for the entire year. That makes little sense. Instead of living with enormous volatility, we need to understand it, at least enough to take a small bite out of it in order to enhance our returns. Knowing that predictable anomalies exist is the first step to establishing that the market itself is predictable.

## CHAPTER NOTES

1. Yale Hirsch and Jeffrey A. Hirsch, *Stock Traders Almanac 2002* (Nyack, NY: Hirsch Organization, 2001), p. 52.
2. Daniel Kahneman, Jack L. Knetsch, and Richard H. Thaler, "Anomalies," in Daniel Kahneman and Amos Tversky (Eds.), *Choices, Values, and Frames* (Cambridge, UK: Cambridge University Press, 2008), p. 159–170.
3. Vijay Singal, *Beyond the Random Walk* (New York: Oxford University Press, 2004), p. 20.
4. Ibid., p. xi.
5. Andrei Shleifer, *Inefficient Markets* (New York: Oxford University Press, 2000).
6. Hirsch and Hirsch, *Stock Traders Almanac 2002*, p.106
7. Singal, *Beyond*, p.26
8. "Stocks & Commodities" V 18:12, Interview: Yale Hirsch: Market Historian, by John Sweeney, December, 2000, p. 68–80.
9. Josef Lakonishok and Seymour Smidt, "Are Seasonal Anomalies Real: A Ninety Year Perspective," *Review of Financial Studies*, 1(4) (Winter 1988): pp. 403–425.
10. Singal, *Beyond*, p. 57.
11. Jeffrey A. Hirsch and J. Taylor Brown, *The Almanac Investor* (New York: Wiley, 2006), p. 98.

12. Mark J. Kamstra, Lisa A. Kramer, and Maurice D. Levi, "Losing Sleep at the Market: The Daylight Saving Anomaly," *American Economic Review*, 90(4) (Sept. 2000): p. 1005.

13. G. William Schwert, "Anomalies and Market Efficiency," National Bureau of Economic Research Working Paper No. W9277, October 2002.

# PART III

# Charting a Golden Path

# A New Market Paradigm 9

*We have now seen the results of many straightforward attempts to document the behavior of stock prices. The results do not conform to the predictions of the theories. They don't even come close. We have two choices. We can advance by developing radically new theories to help us understand what we now see in the data. Or we can go back, denying what is now readily apparent to most, bending the data through even more convoluted econometric processes, until it screams its compliance with our preconceptions.[1]*

ROBERT A. HAUGEN
Professor of Finance at the University of California, Irvine
and author of *The New Finance*

NEW ECONOMIC and social paradigms can take years if not decades to fully materialize, even when their origins are associated with an eventful spark of extraordinary proportion—a war, a major discovery, an economic calamity. The unprecedented events of 2008–09 certainly qualify as the latter. Much of Wall Street, the main protagonist of the current paradigm, has imploded. Our homes, retirement plans, and other major assets have been crushed, as has our confidence in financial institutions, government, regulatory bodies, ratings agencies, and gurus who still cling to the principles that got us where we are today. We are primed for a generational change in thinking about how we view the stock market. This will coincide with another widely anticipated generational occurrence—the passing of an estimated $30 trillion to $40 trillion (or perhaps a lot less now) in baby boomers' wealth to their progeny. I suspect the next generation will be much more open to embracing a new perspective on money and investing.

The collapse of legendary Wall Street firms such as Merrill Lynch, Bear Stearns, and Lehman Brothers (not to mention Fannie Mae, Freddie Mac, and too many banks to list here) demonstrates the power of the 2008 calamity on the financial infrastructure. We relied on these firms for asset management; for financial products meant to serve the needs of investors, corporations, and financial exchanges; and for guidance through a complex financial world in which most individuals are hopelessly lost without professional help. We relied on the government for oversight, and we relied on the news media to keep us informed as financial tragedies unfolded before us in unprecedented speed and scale. In short, we were seriously let down, led to excess, led to believe that things were not as bad as they were, and led astray from the true purpose of investing. Indeed, I'd say the seeds of a new paradigm for the stock market have been sown.

The new paradigm will no doubt usher in material changes to our investment and corporate infrastructure that remedy (or at least address) the weaknesses in the current paradigm, just as occurred in the 1930s. These will likely affect all the major players: investment advisors, brokers, mutual funds, hedge funds, rating agencies, regulatory bodies, financial institutions, and pension managers. Such changes may be legislated while others are self-induced. They are likely to be the subject of many books and articles over the next several years, as well as countless legislative hearings, court proceedings, studies, and debates. Coinciding with these structural changes should be a change in the way we think about stock investing, which should at a minimum include the following acknowledgements:

- Buying stocks in the secondary market is not true investing.
- The price of a stock has two components—fundamental value and subjective value—and the subjective value is arguably the majority of the price we pay for stocks.
- Subjective value is driven by participant behavior and psychology.
- Included in the subjective value of every stock is a contribution of subjective value from the market as a whole in the

form of a premium included in all publicly traded stocks.
Much of this premium is not accounted for at all in classic
financial analysis.

- The fundamentals of a company change very slowly over
  time. Therefore the day-to-day movements we see in stock
  prices are almost entirely driven by behavioral factors.

- The impact of behavioral factors on the stock market gives
  it nonrandom characteristics, making it possible to interpret
  and, to a degree, predict its movements within certain parameters.

- Technical analysis offers one of the best (and only) ways to
  interpret the impact of behavior on stock prices.

- Trend channel analysis, as described herein, offers many
  new insights into the way behavior governs price movements of the forces that drive stocks in general.

- Overreliance on classic financial principles and long-term
  statistics on risk versus return can be hazardous to our
  wealth.

- Overreliance on financial professionals—whose best interests are not necessarily aligned with ours—can also be hazardous to our wealth.

- It is our responsibility as investors to recognize when stocks
  are a good long-term value and when they're not because
  the brokerage and financial management industry cannot be
  relied on to do that for us.

## A TALE OF TWO VALUES

A substantial part of stock investing is predicated on what others are
expected to pay for stocks rather than what they are assumed to be
intrinsically worth. Is that what investing is all about—or is it more
apt to describe a flea market? What we think of as "investing" really
isn't in the pure sense of the word. Buying stocks on the secondary
market is a proxy for investing. I would more accurately term it
*pseudo-investing*. What we get on the secondary market is an interest in the real thing, not an actual physical asset. We can never get
anything physical from the company in which we own shares, not

even in liquidation. We are said to have a claim on the assets and net profits, but we can never actually claim anything that is not paid out as a dividend, and we are the last in line should the company be forced to liquidate. Unless we are majority shareholders, we have virtually no say in how the company is run, who runs it, or what they do with our investment. This essentially renders us "investors once removed."

In a sense, stocks themselves are a derivative. Their value is derived from, but not necessarily a direct reflection of, the financial state of the underlying business. Our ownership interest in a company at any moment is really only worth our share of the book value or share-holders' equity, and stock prices are only loosely pegged to that value—commonly by a multiple of as much as two to five times. That means only a fraction of the price of a stock represents the actual book value of the company. The rest is the premium that we pay for the company's ability to generate future profits on those assets, balanced against the numerous risks they face to both existing assets and future earnings potential. This premium, the majority of the price we pay for a stock, is the part that is highly subjective.

If there were universally accepted parameters for how much a stock was intrinsically worth, given its underlying fundamentals, then we could assume a company's stock price to move up or down in direct relation to those fundamentals. But as discussed throughout this book, there is no single set of such parameters, and the methodologies are neither universal nor constant, resulting in intrinsic values that differ markedly—not just by small fractions but by magnitudes. Furthermore, fundamentals are a moving target, and even the measurements themselves are subject to interpretation. On top of all that, very few market participants, professionals included, actually go to the trouble of examining detailed fundamentals when making buy and sell decisions on stocks. As a result, we know that price may track fundamentals reasonably well over long periods of time but in the interim can disconnect substantially.

Classic finance says that these disconnects are temporary and that they work themselves out over time. I believe that is an excuse for the fact that the classic financial theory has no way to explain it.

If there is going to be a new paradigm, it should deal with reality. The disconnects between stock prices and fundamental value will not go away, and understanding them will make us all better investors. They are not aberrations. They simply don't "fit" into classic theories of stock valuation and therefore require another explanation. That doesn't mean abandoning classic theory for something entirely different; it means combining classic theory with something that explains what it cannot. Financial theory is not useless, just inadequate.

The concept of subjective value, introduced in Chapter 3, suggests that the new paradigm should incorporate a model of stock valuation built around two components of value: fundamental value and subjective value. The fundamental values should be calculated in a straightforward and universal way and without all the subjective multiples that analysts apply to bring them up to market prices. Conservative valuations, more like those of small businesses at three to four times free cash flow, would be more effective. Small businesses may not have economies of scale, but they are also leaner entities and are centered mostly on operations. Large public companies have things like research-and-development departments that may enhance long-term growth prospects but also represent a drag on earnings from ongoing operations. The true bare-bones fundamental or intrinsic value of a company should be tied to its core ongoing operations. The rest, by definition, should be included in the subjective component of its value. The concept is illustrated in **FIGURE 9.1**.

The subjective component can then include all the things that are affected by the perception or the behavioral characteristics of market participants. These would include the impressions investors have of the company and its management, the multiples they are willing to assign to future earnings, and their assessment of all the other risks and uncertainties facing the company. On top of that, the subjective value of any stock must also include the subjective view of the market as a whole, and that likely represents the largest piece of subjective value altogether. The subjective value should also be acknowledged to be independent of fundamental value and to vary over the life of a company as described in Chapter 3.

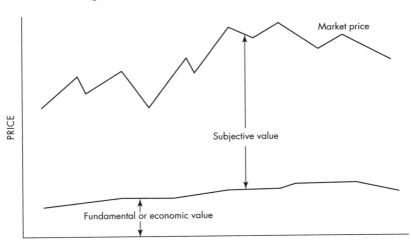

Figure 9.1    An Illustration of Subjective versus Fundamental Value

You may be wondering how we would quantify subjective value. The answer? The market will calculate it for us, and we will simply measure it. The model for this type of valuation already exists with options.

Options have the equivalent of a fundamental value. In short, the fundamental value of any option is called the *theoretical value* and can be calculated at any moment in time. Theoretical value consists of an *intrinsic component* and a *time component*. The intrinsic component is the value that would be realized if the option were to be exercised at this very moment (in other words, the amount by which the option is "in the money" right now, if at all), and the time component is the additional value created by the statistical probability (given the volatility of the underlying stock) that the option will have even more intrinsic value between now and its expiration. The theoretical or fundamental value of an option is accepted by most to be determined by a formula developed by Fischer Black and Myron Scholes. There are a few other option valuation models floating around, but by and large the great majority of the financial community accepts the Black-Scholes valuations as the theoretical value of any option.

While Black-Scholes theoretical values provide a universally accepted benchmark value for any option, market prices for options can differ markedly from this value. The difference is simply referred to as the amount by which an option is over- or undervalued, but it might just as well be termed the *subjective value* of the option. (Option players consider how over- or undervalued an option is by what its *implied volatility* is in comparison to the historic volatility. That's just another way of looking at the same thing.) It is the market's way of saying that the option is worth more or less than the calculated fundamental value. Given that there is an accepted benchmark standard for the fundamental value, we can simply compare that to the actual market price and label the difference, whether positive or negative, as the subject value of the option. If your online broker provides option "chains" (price tables) on their screens, as most do, you will see either the implied volatility, the Black-Scholes theoretical value, or both. Plenty of free Internet sites such as Yahoo! Finance and the Chicago Board Options Exchange's CBOE.com also provide this type of information.

If we were able to calculate an acceptable fundamental value for individual stocks, then we could easily aggregate that to an index like the Dow Jones Industrial Averages or the Standard & Poor's (S&P) 500 Index. At the market level, the subjective value of the index could be viewed as the net weighted subjective values of its components. But at the market level, there are also factors that do not emanate from individual stocks, or that apply to all stocks, and we might ultimately be able to measure these (at least in aggregate) as well.

As we know, calculating fundamental values for stocks is much more challenging and problematic than for options, and there is no single methodology like Black-Scholes that is currently accepted. But we could eventually get there if someone took the initiative to zero in on a single method for calculating fundamental values, at least for this purpose.

## PSEUDO-RANDOM

If we accept the influence of human behavior on stock prices, then the new paradigm should consider an expanded view of the stock market that incorporates a degree of irrationality and semipredictability.

Rather than a black-and-white perspective that describes the market as wholly random or nonrandom, we merely need to accept at least some degree of compromise between these extremes to arrive at a very different perspective on the market than we have currently. That compromise would hold stock prices to be largely random or, if I may be excused for coining my own oxymoron, "deterministically random," and the overall market to exhibit both random and nonrandom characteristics. What I mean by deterministically random is that they are random up to a point, like subatomic particles that move about in random fashion, but remain within the confines of a three-dimensional area that is determined by various physical forces.

This random–nonrandom duality is not uncommon in nature, where many instances of both order and randomness coexist. Tree branches emerge in random directions, yet when fully grown, take on a predictable and orderly size and shape. Birds and fish exhibit random behavior when observed by themselves but orderly behavior in large groups. The stock market is similar: random at the level of minute-to-minute price changes but increasingly more orderly and predictable when aggregated over hours, days, and months.

Others can challenge themselves on verifying (or negating) this supposition with advanced mathematics, but I will outline the intuitive logic behind it. It stands to reason that momentary changes in stock prices are essentially random. Supply and demand represent independent variables, and minute-to-minute (or second-to-second) price changes reflect the asynchronous nature of supply and demand as it varies throughout the day. Specialists or market makers provide a bid–ask quote with a spread that reflects their desire to make a profit for their role as intermediaries. Thus, as transactions come in during the trading day, most of these transactions likely execute at either the bid or the offer, depending on whether they are buys or sells; and as discussed earlier, most participants, including institutions, demand an immediacy of execution. On that basis, the price of a stock should at least vary randomly between the bid and the offer (or slightly outside that spread as large transactions are accommodated). Order volume tends to be stronger at the beginning and end of the trading day, but during the in-between hours order arrival may be determined as much by the vagaries of lunch hours across different time zones or the need to meet a tee time as any kind of prescribed financial behavior. In sum, momentary price changes tend to be driven by the serendipity of order flow rather than by longer-term strategic or value decisions and are understandably random.

In the big picture, however, the dynamics change. Over the course of hours and days, news arrives that affects companies, their competitors, the economic climate, and all the other factors that affect buy and sell decisions. Participants assess the news, determine the likely impact on stocks, and make decisions accordingly. At this level, price changes themselves actually impact buy and sell decisions. Some who see the price rising may want to jump on, while others may seize the opportunity to sell. In other words, price movement in the stock itself (or in others) isn't just the result of supply and demand, it causes changes in supply and demand. This is a different perspective than that assumed by traditional economics, which is based on the notion that supply and demand are independent variables. In a classic supply–demand scenario, diminished supply forces buyers who need that item to pay more for it. As the price rises, there is pressure on those who need the item to purchase less. But in the stock world, there is a notably different psychology at work. Many buyers who see other buyers purchasing a stock actually view that as a reason to buy and pay more (see "Herding" in Chapter 7). This is a grave distortion of standard supply–demand logic.

In *Predictably Irrational*, Ariely writes,

> As our experiments demonstrate, what consumers are willing to pay can easily be manipulated, and this means that consumers don't in fact have a good handle on their own preferences and the prices they are willing to pay for different goods and experiences. Second, whereas the standard economic framework assumes that the forces of supply and demand are independent . . . anchoring manipulations we have shown here suggest that they are, in fact, dependent. It seems, then, that instead of consumers' willingness to pay influencing market prices, the causality is somewhat reversed and it is market prices themselves that influence consumers' willingness to pay.[2]

Furthermore, in the case of stocks, causality can move demand in the opposite direction that classic economics would anticipate—buying can beget buying, and a rising price can actually create new demand. This is further fed by the activity of short sellers, who will need to buy as prices rise in order to limit potential losses or lock in gains. The concept of shorting and short covering are unique characteristics of the stock market and are nonexistent in the classic economic supply–demand construct.

The market begins to show definable trends in time periods as small as hours. These become more pronounced in terms of days and weeks but are noticeably less defined for individual stocks and appear mostly at the industry sector or market level. The majority of the movement in a stock comes from the market, but individual stocks are subject to things particular to a company or industry. Apple stock falls when Steve Jobs becomes ill but then rallies when a positive economic statistic comes forth and the market rises overall. These are different parameters entirely. Being driven by more subjective matters (such as perception of the economy, a new administration, or flare-ups on the world geopolitical scene) and by the need to put money to use in—or to reduce exposure to—equities, the market can be argued to be more behaviorally influenced and thus more likely to exhibit a predictable character. In addition, the market audience is huge enough for the random actions of individuals to be statistically negated, leaving the overall price movement to more accurately reflect underlying group behavior.

### Adding Behavior to the Mix

There is no item of greater importance to the new paradigm than the acceptance of behavioral factors as an ever-present force in secondary financial markets. We need to dismiss the notion that behavioral factors represent nothing more than irrelevant noise in the movement of stock prices or that they are irrational anomalies that are counteracted by well-informed professionals. Instead, we must accept that they are systematic, significant, and permanent contributors to price movement. Acceptance, however, means nothing if not accompanied by ways in which we can use that information to develop and implement investment strategy more successfully.

So how do we add behavior to the mix?

Even with perfect knowledge of a company's fundamentals, we know there is no formula for determining the market price (or, as discussed earlier, the intrinsic value) of a stock. Likewise, behavioral factors are so varied, so complex, and so dynamic that they could not possibly be quantified for every participant in the market or even for the major groups of participants. Even if they could, we would need to assess the mood of the market constantly in order to get the data for such a model. Clearly, approaching behavior from the perspective of the participants and somehow using that information to predict stock or market prices is unrealistic. We therefore have little alternative but to look in the opposite direction—to examine the market's behavior and attempt to understand what it is telling us about the participants. We examine the market's behavior through price charts and other forms of technical analysis. If the market is indeed random, then we will not find anything useful. But if behavior is a valid contributor to stock prices, then it is likely we will find valuable clues. Those of us who use technical analysis have been observing behavioral clues since before we even knew exactly what we were observing.

The participants in financial markets are natural creatures, and that renders the markets themselves, to at least some degree, natural phenomena. Like other natural phenomena, the market's action is governed by a number of variables, interacting in complex ways to produce a continually changing outcome. Those variables typically have a "normal" range of values that they not only exhibit most of the time but also have the ability to reach extreme values on rare occasions. I find weather to represent a good analogy. The primary variables in weather—temperature, humidity, wind, precipitation, air pressure—are ever present, and the weather on any given day is determined by the relative values and interactions of these factors. On days in which no single factor stands out, the weather exists in a "normal" range, governed largely by location and season. But when any one or more of these variables exceeds its range of values, it can drive the weather far outside its normal variance, creating extreme weather scenarios such as hurricanes, droughts, floods, and tornadoes.

In similar fashion, it may be that the impact of behavior during normal market conditions is relatively benign and overtakes the influence of financials only at extremes. Due to the number of people involved in the U.S. stock market and the number of different behavioral factors that we already know to have at least some effect on our financial decisions, the way in which behavioral factors influence price is likely to be overwhelmingly complex and may defy quantification. Even if we could quantify behavior based on past factors, we would not be able to assume it would work that way with new, never-before-experienced factors. No model, for example, could have accurately anticipated the effect of 9/11 since nothing like that had ever occurred before. Therefore, even attempting to arrive at some kind of pricing model from individual behavioral factors is going to represent a task of indescribable complexity. We need, instead, to let the market tell us what the effect is. Our challenge is to figure out how to read and interpret the behavior from the market as it happens, and many who utilize technical analysis have already done that.

Our behavior as a group has been read, measured, and interpreted many times before. Everything we buy is affected by our behavioral nature. We consider purchases of food, cosmetics, and electronics to be consumer goods, but our behavior as consumers is not limited to these items. It affects literally everything we buy, including cars, houses, insurance, art, and stocks. The same behavior involved in rushing out to buy an iPhone when it first debuted is evident in those who rushed to buy Google stock when it first went public. We are influenced by news and PR in the same way we are influenced by advertising. In fact, advertising forms our impression of many public companies, and there is no reason why that cannot be expected to carry over into stock purchases.

## GETTING TECHNICAL

If we are going to adopt a new perspective on the stock market that incorporates behavior as a key aspect of pricing, then we must embrace technical analysis as currently the most practical way of understanding how behavior manifests itself in stock prices. We must acknowledge that it is not an exact science and that we will most likely want to employ multiple aspects of technical analysis (just as there are multiple types of fundamental analysis) but that overall it will be an indispensable tool.

In this new paradigm, many will realize what technical analysts and followers have known for quite some time—that the indicators tell us something about the story of what's going on across the vast universe of market participants. Interpretation is often the key because the tool is not always able to give us precise or unequivocal information. By knowing the behavior and psychology of the participants, we are much better able to match the technical signs with underlying behavior. Nontechnicians tend to view trend analysis as just a way of knowing something about what is happening right now and of no use in forecasting the future. But technicians have known all along that the numbers and charts represent important insights into the underlying behavior of market participants and can tell us about trends or changes in behavior.

Take the CBOE's Volatility Index (VIX), for example—a technical indicator that measures the premiums on S&P 500 options. Option premiums react to supply and demand like anything else; when the market declines, institutions and professional money managers look to protect their portfolios by purchasing put options on the S&P 500. While some may lighten their positions in stocks, buying the puts is a much easier and quicker way to ensure a portfolio's downside than buying and selling a small portion of, say, fifty to 100 different stocks whenever the market dips. In addition, managers must be mindful of tax and transaction-cost implications, not to mention the fact that their own selling would tend to exacerbate existing price erosion. So they turn to S&P 500 puts for downside protection. Heightened demand for puts increases the premiums, and the VIX reflects this by rising in value. Thus, this indicator links directly to a specific behavioral factor: fear of a market decline. Heightened demand for puts causes premiums to expand on the puts, and arbitrage carries those price increases over to the calls as well. The VIX backs off as the market advances, as the need for insuring the downside dissipates. Demand for call index options, by the way, does not occur in the same manner when the market is expected to rise since portfolio managers are already long equities and do not tend to leverage themselves further with call options. This has aptly earned VIX the title of the "fear gauge" in the media.

The VIX tends to rise in market declines and fall during advances, thus making it a coincident indicator and not specifically a leading or predictive indicator. But it is useful in helping to determine, for example, when an up day inside of a longer downtrend is being perceived by institutions as a turning point (strong drop in VIX) or simply a bounce within a still-declining trend (very little drop, if any). In addition, VIX has futures, which can be used as a leading indicator when they trade at a significant discount or premium to the current VIX price.

Other technical indicators also provide important clues to underlying behavior or perceptions. The short-term trading index (TRIN), developed by Richard W. Arms Jr. and also sometimes referred to as the *Arms Index*, measures the ratio of the number of advancing over declining issues to the volume in the advancers over the volume in the decliners. The TRIN tends to be helpful in confirming market bottoms when its readings become excessively high (say, 1.3 or higher) because such levels tend to signify the type of indiscriminate selling that accompanies market bottoms. Moving averages tend to smooth out short-term volatility and reveal underlying trends. A technique pioneered by Gerald Appel uses *moving average convergence–divergence* (MACD) to determine when a shorter-term moving average is crossing over a longer-term moving average, suggesting that a trend is changing direction.

A prevalent view of trend analysis holds that it is the province of traders and is not geared to the longer term horizon of "investors." On this I could not disagree more. While it is essential for short-term traders, it can be equally valuable for investors with any time horizon. Its use would be justified with even just one technical signal in years of investing that indicated a major market turn. Without any technical aid in decision making, one is doomed to be a long-term buy-and-hold investor with no way to exit the market except as a result of no longer being able to stand the pain of loss.

## WAGGING THE DOG

In the new paradigm, our attention will move further away from stocks and toward sectors or market indexes. If, as postulated earlier in this chapter and in Chapter 3, the majority of the volatility in a portfolio of individual stocks is actually a function of the volatility in the overall market, and if we can more accurately read the market's behavior than the more erratic behavior of individual stocks, then there is little reason other than pure speculation to buy individual stocks. In this sense, classic portfolio theory is right on the money with its principle of diversifying away the risks inherent in individual stocks. Individual stocks are fraught with issues—bad management, insider trading, employee stock options, and a ton of things they keep from the public but act on themselves. Portfolio theory states that, statistically, there is an equal chance of good news from a stock as bad, and that these occurrences essentially negate each other in large numbers of stocks. This theory, however, was arrived at using top-down mathematics, not by observing a large number of actual portfolios. As such, the dynamics are different. If you own a portfolio and you hold it through thick and thin, then the numbers may work out. But if you are actually taking positions in individual stocks, you may not realize the same results, and you would be influenced to sell prematurely when stocks make unpredictable moves. Since it is in a company's best interests to tout good news and suppress bad news, its disclosures may not be as forthcoming as an investor might like.

On the other hand, vehicles such as index funds and exchange-traded funds (ETFs) now abound for investing in the market or in major sectors. They even exist for the overall markets of other countries. With informative and practical techniques for reading the market, we can put capital to use in these vehicles using whatever time horizon we are comfortable with—from very short-term trading to long-term investing. We don't need to anguish over the fundamentals or the vagaries of individual stock moves or try to make ourselves into macroeconomists. We can simply read the charts and act accordingly. And if our aim is to buy and hold for the long term, then at least we have a mechanism for determining when the potential dangers are getting too great even for long-term comfort.

This book has suggested that the overall market, as defined by averages such as the Dow Jones Industrial Averages and the S&P 500, may be more affected by behavioral factors than by the fundamentals of individual stocks and therefore exhibits a more readily interpreted signature of movement. Literally, every market participant watches the Dow or S&P in addition to whatever equities they specifically own. These averages are the universal benchmarks used by investment managers throughout the world. They are ubiquitous and repeatedly enter into investment decisions, even when considering individual stocks. They are blasted all over the media. People pick up market quotes on their cell phones. In everyone's mind, they *are* the market. Now that these and other indexes and averages have effectively been securitized into ETFs or through derivatives such as options and futures, they are even more firmly embedded into our psyches.

At the market level, there is a sentiment factor that comes into play. That sentiment factor intermixes with the performance of all individual stocks combined. Whether the sentiment component drives individual stock prices or whether it is independent, it nonetheless exists. News pundits regularly ascribe the market's daily movements to something that happened that day. Most of the time, the daily rationale according to the press is whatever news item happens to coincide with market direction. When the news is about an individual stock, the pundits justify their market calls by applying "bellwether" status to that company. If there is no particular news item that appears to explain the day's activity, then the pundits simply tap what they believe to be the market's overall background concerns. Generalized explanations like "concerns about inflation" or "worries about the effect of higher oil prices" are given.

Movements also frequently occur at the market level as a result of institutional activity such as index arbitrage and activities related to ETFs. This can often create demand to either buy or sell a large basket of stocks in substantial volume and thus impact market movement. The increasing demand for ETFs and the arbitrage activities that accompany it will only serve to increase the focus on market indexes even more. To understand market movements in the new paradigm, investors will need to understand the effect these instruments have on the behavior of the underlying stocks they represent.

## COMING TO GRIPS WITH MONEY MANAGEMENT

In the new paradigm, significant structural changes should take place in the money-management business. At the very least, people should be aware of several important facts. The first of these is that the investment-management and brokerage industries do not exist to maximize our wealth, minimize our risks, or see that the financial system works effectively for all parties involved. It is like any other service industry—governed by a profit motive and constrained by the practical limitations of providing a complex set of services to millions of people and tens of thousands of institutions. The brokerage industry, bank trust departments, financial planners, and independent money managers cannot truly give one-on-one service except to megaclients with tens of millions of dollars. They may spend time with the client in the beginning to make sure they get the client into a program that fits, but after that the client can expect to be on autopilot.

As long as the industry is compensated by asset-management fees that are unrelated to performance, it will direct its actions to asset gathering and pay only enough attention to performance as is necessary to remain within accepted peer benchmarks. Money managers will continue to manage portfolios in cost-effective, universally applied manner, which will be as highly automated and decision free as they can make it. You can expect to see less and less stock picking and more and more ETFs in your portfolio, along with more automatically rebalanced accounts that simply apply an asset allocation to your account via computer. That is the safe and practical road for money managers: in their best interests, not yours.

CHAPTER NOTES

1. Robert A. Haugen, *The New Finance: The Case Against Efficient Markets* (New York: Prentice Hall, 1995), p. 137.
2. Dan Ariely, *Predictably Irrational* (New York: HarperCollins, 2008), p. 45.

# Introduction to Trend Channel Analysis

**10**

*Although it is always perilous to assume that the future will be like the past, it is at least instructive to find out what the past was like.*

WILLIAM F. SHARPE, Nobel Laureate

BEHAVIOR IS A rather amorphous and unquantifiable variable for any single individual, let alone millions of market participants. Consequently, knowing that human behavior affects the markets is somewhat useless without having a way of interpreting or measuring it at the market level. So, the question before us is how do we actually accomplish that?

The answer lies in technical market analysis and charting. Knowing that investors are strongly prone to exhibit common heuristics and biases in their thinking—and that their judgments and actions are affected by a plethora of unconscious efforts, such as herding, anchoring, and overconfidence—there is good reason to accept that what price charts communicate is the "signature" on the market that is imposed by the participants. More simply, if the charts depict the action of the market and market action reflects the aggregate behavior of the participants, then participant behavior is reflected in the charts, and our challenge is to interpret it.

Price charts provide a plethora of visual cues and can be analyzed in numerous ways. Although prices change continually, the way they change over time (e.g., the market's cyclical ebb and flow, the angles and degrees of ascent and descent, and the subsequent patterns formed) reflects the unique nature and characteristics of all the participants. Prechter has been saying this for years using Elliott wave analysis to link social mood with market action.

The countless variables that affect our decisions to buy and sell stocks change constantly, creating the opportunity for different reactions in different circumstances. What is most definitely a "buy" now may be a "sell" in five minutes. It therefore makes intuitive sense that even if investors are looking at behavior when they read a chart, they would not be able to predict the next price from that information. Chart reading is not about precise prediction. It's about interpreting what's going on, understanding that behavior tends to move within certain parameters, and, most importantly, understanding the basic trend of the market, both in the short and longer time frames. It's about determining the likelihood of price moving in a certain magnitude and direction from the current moment. If stocks were totally random, then we would not be able to do that with any better than 50–50 results, but the charts tell us otherwise. They show us direction, and they give us boundaries that contain moves with compelling consistency and often startling accuracy. If an investor can improve the 50–50 chance of just getting direction right, then that alone will give them an enormous advantage over the herd.

### TRENDS AND CHANNELS

The concept of a trend—whether in home values, fashion, or weather—is one that is familiar to most people, though a specific description of a trend is elusive. Dictionary definitions are invariably vague, describing trends with phrases such as "general direction" or "prevailing tendency." When the term is applied to stock or commodity prices, it takes on a more quantitative character, but there is still no universal definition. Yet there is clear consensus on the importance of trends. As John Murphy, the author of several books on technical analysis, states, "The concept of a trend is absolutely essential to the technical approach to market analysis. All of the tools used by the chartist—support and resistance levels, price patterns, moving averages, trend lines, etc.—have the sole purpose of helping to measure the trend of the market for the purpose of participating in that trend."[1]

Stock trends have been defined in many different ways by different authors. Charles Dow referred to them as *movements*. R. N. Elliott and Robert Prechter call them *waves*. Still others refer to them as *cycles*, *bands*, or *envelopes*. Trends are defined by single trend or regression line, multiple trend lines, moving averages, or curvilinear bands. In all these situations, the concept of a trend is similar, but the details and parameters are often unique to the source. A common characteristic of most trend types is that they can be viewed in different time periods, with shorter trends frequently "nesting" inside longer ones, but the time periods differ with the technique employed.

As the writings of Charles Dow attest, chartists have observed for more than a century that the meanderings of stocks take on certain visual characteristics—zigzag patterns over periods of days, cyclical ebb and flow patterns over weeks and months, and a steady upward bias over years to decades. **FIGURES 10.1**, **10.2**, and **10.3** show this perspective in charts of the Standard & Poor's (S&P) 500 Index (SPX).

In longer time periods (Figures 10.2 and 10.3), the charts strongly suggest up trends, but the conclusion is more ambiguous in the shorter time period (Figure 10.1). Clearly, for the concept of a trend to be useful, the chartist has to have specific rules and parameters to apply.

Channels remove the vagueness in charts and provide explicit determinations of direction. They transform charts like those on the next page into road maps that can be interpreted, followed, and projected. They also take a subjective image and enable you to extract actionable conclusions from it.

The methodology for creating trend channels that is chronicled in this book is trend channel analysis (TCA). In TCA, trend channels are defined by two parallel lines that form a boundary above and below the data for a given time period or parts of it. But in contrast to the traditional view of trend channels as stray occurrences

Figure 10.1    SPX Three-Day Chart

Source: StockCharts.com

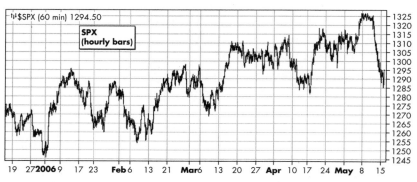

Figure 10.2    SPX Six-Month Chart

Source: StockCharts.com

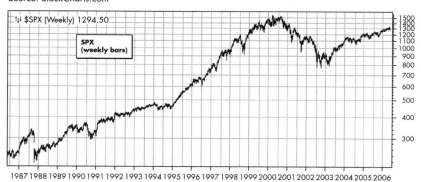

Figure 10.3    SPX Twenty-Year Chart

Source: StockCharts.com

like triangles, rising wedges, and head-and-shoulders formations—patterns that are useful when observed but only present on occasion—TCA is a continuously available tool like moving averages, momentum oscillators, and Elliott waves.

To illustrate the basics of drawing trend channels, **FIGURE 10.4** shows the same three-day chart of the SPX as in Figure 10.1 but with channels drawn. Even in this brief period of barely twenty trading hours, there are three distinct trend channels as indicated by the circled numbers on the chart. Each of these three channels forms a leg within larger channel 4, which encompasses the whole three-day period. Beginning with channels like these lasting only a matter of hours, a road map begins to take shape. (In any particular time view, I refer to the channels inside larger channels as *mini-channels*.) Channels that small are significant enough (these are each about 1.8% of the SPX) to provide trading opportunities for professional traders or nimble investors, but their big advantage lies in their ability to build the larger road map and provide early clues or affirmations of changes in the direction of larger channels.

Points A and B in Figure 10.4 are noted for their importance in changes to trend direction. When SPX broke channel 1 (changed direction) on the morning of May 14, it came back to touch the same channel line at about 11 a.m. (point A) before advancing again. The same break-and-retest pattern occurred in the opposite direction

Figure 10.4    SPX Three-Day Chart with Channels

Source: StockCharts.com

when the SPX broke down from channel 2 later that same day, coming back to touch the channel line at around 11 a.m. on May 15 before declining further. This break-and-retest pattern is very common among channels of all sizes and helps confirm that a channel has actually broken (more on channel breaks in Chapter 11).

Perhaps the most profound implication of TCA is that it provides an intuitive link to the behavioral conclusions that have been brought to light. Anchoring and herding, for example, help explain why trend channels form and persist. They might also help us understand why channel boundary lines can be uncannily precise at times, with the market reversing direction at the exact point of touching a trend boundary—something that should happen on rare occasion in a random market. The fact that the channels appear to work much better at the market level than for individual stocks has a logical basis in participant behavior. Individual stocks have a relatively narrow audience and are more easily influenced by news, rumors, and often one-sided supply or demand. Market moves, on the other hand, are the result of the behavior of hundreds of thousands or even millions of participants. As with large portfolios of stocks, the large number of constituents removes the statistical randomness of individual actions, leaving overarching group-driven considerations to rule price action.

In addition, as continuously available tools, trend channels can now be used in a much more comprehensive way than simply to jump on a short-term trend in progress for a quick trade. Important inflection points occur at the intersection of short- and long-term channels. These inflection points can represent major turning points in the market, with strong implications for longer-term investors. The slope and width of a channel provide valuable clues as to whether a market move is likely to be quick and unsustainable or whether it has the makings of something more substantial.

The connection between participant behavior and the trend channels is a highly significant one. It is also a highly complex one that should not be taken to mean the market is going to fall into perfectly predictable patterns that are 100-percent reliable. After all, it is based on human behavior. But by using a defined set of rules and assumptions, we can represent and interpret the market's action visually and learn a great deal from the resulting picture about both short- and long-term trends, moves within those trends, the slope and strength of those trends, and potential points where the market will have a higher probability of changing direction. Anyone who follows the stock market should appreciate the power of that type of information.

## HOW THEY WORK

The way TCA works is to draw channels on recent or historic market data, both in short- and long-term time frames, and use the current pattern to project where the channels (or legs within those channels) are currently headed. I use twenty-day charts with five-minute bars, forty-day charts with hourly bars, and one-year or three-year charts with daily bars to get the complete picture. (Figures 10.1 to 10.3 typify the views from these three time periods.) In reality, we cannot know for sure where any channel is going in advance, but knowing that the market continuously channels and knowing when a channel is breaking or changing, we can make valid projections very early in any channel's development. It is important to then recognize that the market is not guaranteed to do anything and that our projections may certainly change as a channel progresses. Once you have either the first two peaks or troughs, you can draw a preliminary channel, and since the first leg of a new channel is generally the last leg of the prior one, you can get a look at a short-term channel in a day or two that might end up lasting ten to twenty days or more. You can get big clues from the individual legs of a short-term channel, which often form channels themselves (mini-channels), which you can forecast with accuracy within a few hours. That said, the earlier one can project a preliminary channel, the more likely that channel will need to be adjusted along the way.

The trend channel technique has almost no time limitations; it has been effective in time frames ranging from hours to years. One of its major benefits is the ability to identify trends within as little as a few hours of market data and to identify or confirm critical breaks and changes in direction literally in minutes. This makes it one of the most timely indicators in technical analysis.

There is a bit of an art to drawing channels as they are just beginning. Until a channel has at least three to four legs, the channel boundary lines will not be parallel to a regression line through the data. Working with channels, there will therefore be times when a chartist will have much more confidence in the patterns than others. This is to be expected and important to acknowledge.

### BECOMING A CHANNELIST

Trend channel analysis defines a channel by drawing lines above and below a data series that are parallel to each other and to the trend itself (as would be indicated by a standard linear regression line for that data series), touching the highest and lowest data points in the trend (those farthest from the center of the trend), and thus containing all data points in the series. To minimally define a channel, at least one of the two lines must connect two points in the data series. If the line connecting the two farthest points from center is not parallel to the trend, then chances are that the chartist is either including too much of the time series and is mixing parts of two channels or is not including enough of the time series to see the entire channel. Neither case is a valid channel scenario.

The importance of stipulating these requirements is to prevent us from assuming a predictive nature to a time series where none is evident. In other words, if a time series isn't properly channeling, then it is not likely to provide a reliable forecast on future action. In general, it is important to impose a discipline on the observer by forcing him or her to find a valid channel or to remain unbiased until one emerges. In five years of using this technique, I have never been in the position of being completely unable to draw a channel on a major stock index that meets the qualifications, except at the mini-channel level. On some sectors and on most individual stocks, one may frequently see data that does not appear to channel, which tells us that other factors are influencing price and that TCA may simply not be a reliable technique in that situation. It is better to accept the limitations of the technique than to fabricate channels where they don't otherwise exist and risk false signals.

When observed as an occasional occurrence, a trend channel is not even likely to be recognized until quite well defined, thereby limiting the potential benefit to be gained from trading it at that point in time. Once we treat channels as continuous entities, however, and we know that the end of one channel ushers in the beginning of a new one, we can anticipate the new channel. Frequently, the last leg of the channel that's ending becomes the first leg of the new one. This overlap becomes a huge advantage to chartists as it enables us to draw preliminary new channels very early in their existence, reaping far more benefit as a result. Therefore, in TCA one begins by drawing the channels on a current time series and then adding to or modifying the channels as new price data becomes available. (More specific rules for drawing trend channel lines are presented in Chapter 11.)

To illustrate, **FIGURES 10.5, 10.6, 10.7,** and **10.8** show charts on the Nasdaq (EA) 100 (QQQQ) over a twenty-day period in April–May 2009 using five-minute price bars. Figure 10.5 shows the raw data for this period without any trend lines.

Figure 10.6 shows the trend lines drawn to indicate the current channel. Figure 10.7 shows the progression of the QQQQ through May 7 and the break in trend. A preliminary new down channel is

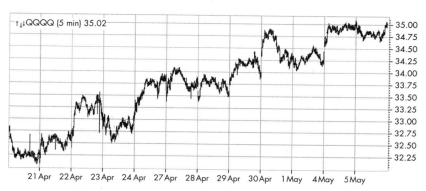

Figure 10.5   QQQQ Two-Week Chart

Source: StockCharts.com

**Figure 10.6   QQQQ Two-Week Chart with Channel**

Source: StockCharts.com

**Figure 10.7   QQQQ Two-Week Chart with Channel Break**

Source: StockCharts.com

drawn on the first day of that trend break. Figure 10.8 shows the index five days later.

## THE PROOF IS IN THE PUDDING

The evidence from Figures 10.7 and 10.4 shows how trend channel analysis can be strikingly accurate in projecting market moves, and the down channel in Figure 10.8 further demonstrates how accurately the data adheres to channels once they are formed. Examples such as these are common occurrences in market action and can be used time and time again as channels form, break, and form again over time.

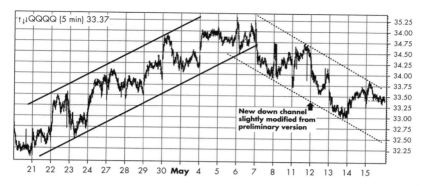

Figure 10.8   SPX Two-Week Chart with Two Channels

Source: StockCharts.com

The overriding factor that makes trend channel analysis such a powerful tool is the discovery that the market not only moves in discrete trend channels but also does so continuously, moving back and forth from up channels to down channels, in both short- and long-term time frames. Until now, trend channels were a very intermittent, hit-or-miss affair. That inconsistency (which I still find exists for most individual stocks) rendered trend analysis unreliable and thus essentially unusable. The only time you could confidently identify a channel was after the fact. This is a problem with almost every type of chart pattern that technicians observe—by the time you notice an intermittent pattern and it develops enough for you to have confidence in its path, it is usually too late to act on it. In addition, you would have to be on the lookout across many securities to spot patterns and would be consequently jumping from one security to the next in order to capitalize on them when they did appear. With TCA, however, you can have confidence very early on because you can project the beginning of the next channel from the end of the prior one, and you can realize significant benefits to trading strategies as a result.

## CHAPTER NOTE

1. John J. Murphy, *Technical Analysis of the Financial Markets* (New York: New York Institute of Finance, 1999), p. 49.

# Reading Between the Lines  11

*Extensive research in what may be termed human activities indicates that practically all developments which result from our social-economic processes follow a law that causes them to repeat themselves in similar and constantly recurring serials of waves or impulses of definite number and pattern.*[1]

RALPH N. ELLIOTT

THE OLD NOTION of a trend channel is little more than that of an isolated formation one could attempt to exploit for a reasonably short-term trade. A technician who spotted one early enough in its formation would attempt to profit by initiating the trade as early as possible in the formation of the channel and exiting the trade when the channel finally "broke" (the point at which the underlying stock or index trades outside of a boundary line in the opposite direction of the trend). There was no way to evaluate the strength of the channel (i.e., its sustainability) or to establish any idea about what might happen following a break. An investor could simply ride the trend for however long it lasted and hope that it continued long enough to make a profit.

Trend channel analysis (TCA) expands this notion immeasurably, transforming trend channels from an occasional one-time exercise in pattern recognition to a continual and dynamic mechanism for evaluating and interpreting the movements of the underlying instrument. A chartist using TCA can follow a particular index on a continual basis, projecting the likely future path of a channel or the likelihood of a channel break or change in slope. That provides a virtually continuous stream of trading opportunities as well as long-term assessment of the underlying potential for hedging strategies as well as strategic accumulation or distribution needs.

When looking for a trend channel as a stand-alone event, a chart viewer would never know where one might begin or end. But knowing that the channels exist on major market indexes on a continual basis, a chartist can draw preliminary channels even before new price data is fully available and then modify the channel as new data appears. In doing so, the technique provides extremely early clues to channel opportunities, likely resistance points, trend breaks, changes in trend slope, and potential risks. Since TCA is predicated on the idea that channels result from participant behavior, and since behavior, even at a group level, can change frequently, TCA recognizes that channels can (and do) change in midstream, and it captures those changes almost as fast as they occur.

## THE GUIDELINES

For consistent development of a methodology with a defined structure, a strict set of rules and assumptions are necessary. Only in this manner can the technique be applied across different underlying securities or markets and across different time periods with a high degree of confidence. A consistent methodology also provides a means of back testing the approach on past data and ultimately being able to quantify the probability of future success. With that in mind, the main tenets of TCA may be summarized as follows:

1.  The stock market's price action is characterized by discrete directional movements referred to as *trend channels*. Trend channels are continuous—in other words, the market always moves back and forth in a channel, even during extreme movements.

2.  The back-and-forth movements inside a channel are called *legs*. Channel legs tend to alternate between the two boundaries of the channel but not always. A strong channel

leg (generally at the end of a channel) can "push" the existing boundary lines in the direction of the trend, causing a trend channel to either widen or change slope.

3. Channels are always bounded by parallel lines. These boundary lines must be drawn (and accordingly modified) to always contain all the data points (price movements) in the time period.

4. For common reference, there are three levels of channels: long-term channels (lasting months to years), short-term channels (days and weeks), and mini-channels (hours). Hourly channels form the legs of short-term channels, and short-term channels form the legs of long-term channels. When viewing a long-term trend, the short-term channels will appear as the mini-channels.

5. Channels oscillate between up movements and down or sideways movements, with periodicity, slope, size (width), and duration all varying.

6. Channels overlap. The last leg of one is frequently the first leg of the next.

7. Breaks of channels in the opposite direction of the channel (i.e., an upward trending channel breaking its lower boundary line) indicate either a deceleration (flattening in slope) or a trend reversal. Breaks of channel boundaries in the existing direction of the channel (i.e., an up-trending channel breaking its upper boundary) indicate trend acceleration or steepening of the slope. Accelerations are far less common than flattenings and reversals.

8. Channels frequently change slope (bend), and narrow or widen while continuing in the same direction.

9. Channel lines often provide precise levels of support and resistance for market moves.

10. Channels are not absolute. They are reflective of how market participants are acting as a group and embody their fickle nature accordingly.

11. Channels tell us where participant action is currently taking the market—whether that agrees with our own views or not.

The tenets above are not meant to imply scientific certainty but to represent a technique for reading and interpreting a natural phenomenon with some degree of consistency. To put it more simply, the technique is subject to interpretation and is best applied when viewed under the above guidelines. More specific channel characteristics are identified below.

### BOUNDARY LINES

Trend channel boundary lines must be parallel. If the lines connecting the highest peaks and lowest troughs are not parallel, then one or both are incorrectly drawn. If there are three points either above or below and they are not in a straight line, then two are correct (or possibly only one) and the other is not. When I have difficulty determining which points to connect, I consider several possibilities and may also use the linear regression line through the data series as a guide. (The regression line, also called the *least squares line* in statistics, can usually be drawn or calculated with a simple tool on Stockcharts.com or by using other chart software.)

The boundary lines must contain all data in the channel. I rarely allow data to fall outside a channel line under the label of what is known as a *throw over* or *false break*. When it happens, the preferable approach is to move the line to accommodate the data. Otherwise, you'll end up making subjective decisions about where the channel lines actually are, and that leads to unreliability.

**FIGURE 11.1** is an example of a correct trend channel analysis chart. The lines are parallel, and at least one (if not two) lines connect two

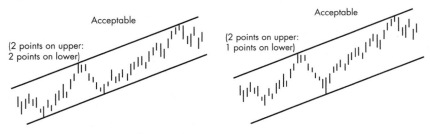

Figure 11.1   Acceptable Channel Boundary Lines

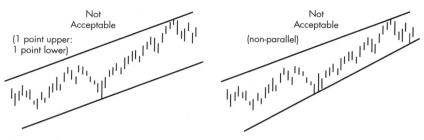

Figure 11.2    Unacceptable Channel Boundary Lines

points. **FIGURE 11.2** is an example of unacceptable channels that have only one point on both lines or have nonparallel lines. Why must boundary lines be parallel? When lines are not parallel on a given time series, there are two reasons that explain almost all such occurrences: (1) the time series is not complete, and ultimately the price points will come up to meet the parallel line later on—a very important thing to know when you are following channels; or (2) what you are really seeing is the boundaries of two different channels overlapping—also something you want to be aware of. Whenever I've drawn a channel as a triangle or pennant, I almost invariably end up proven wrong at a later time.

### TRIANGULAR FORMATIONS

Triangles may appear in trend channels, but they are not substitutes for parallel channels. If the line that connects the peaks is not parallel to the line that connects the troughs, then only one will prove to be an actual channel boundary. The other will prove to be the boundary of an overlapping or larger channel or something else. (Triangular formations occur most often when a mini-channel is approaching a larger channel boundary and the index gets "squeezed" between them by opposing forces.) **FIGURE 11.3** is a time series with a triangular formation (lines A and B). When encountering this situation, it is best to assume that a parallel channel exists but that we do not know which line is the true channel boundary. Either the A line or the B line will ultimately prove false, but at this point you would not know which one. Keeping two channels alive as alternate scenarios

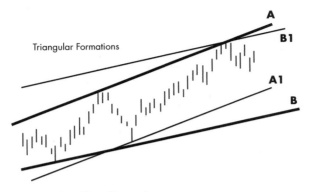

Figure 11.3   Triangular Chart Formations

is advised when that happens. That way, one tends to keep an open mind about the two possibilities until the real one proves itself. Therefore, I draw alternates A1 and B1 parallel to both the original lines and keep both options open until one proves incorrect. In the end, a parallel channel almost always becomes visible.

### A SAMPLE CHART

**FIGURE 11.4** illustrates a short-term trend channel on the Energy Select (XLE) Spider (Standard & Poor's Depositary Receipts). Points A and B define the upper line, while D, E, and F define the lower line. Even though point C is a higher price point than A and B, it is only higher from the chart's perspective, not from the *trend's* perspective. If you were to draw a regression or least squares line through the center of the trend, you would see that A and B are farther from that center line than C. Also, if you were to draw the upper line between points B and C instead of A, then you would immediately see that the line is neither parallel to the lower line or the trend itself, rendering it incorrect as the channel boundary. The fact that point C did not reach the upper channel boundary actually provides an important clue that the trend was losing momentum and weakening. Sure enough, two days later, on February 11, the XLE Spider fell below the lower channel boundary, breaking the short-term channel and suggesting that a new tentative down channel was now forming as shown.

Figure 11.4   Energy Select (XLE) Sector Spider Twenty-Day Chart

Source: StockCharts.com

The amazing thing about these channels is that multiple points hit the lines exactly. If the data were distributed in a random fashion, then we would expect the extreme data points to fall at different distances from the center, statistically described by a normal distribution or something similar. If that were the case, then lines would rarely be parallel (our study shows about 1 percent of the time), yet we observe parallel lines to occur repeatedly and with surprising precision.

## CHANNEL BREAKS

Channel breaks are important to anticipate as accurately as possible as they will frequently engender a trading action. (That is another reason I try to remain as disciplined as possible on drawing the channels—so I can identify when a break is occurring as quickly as possible.) In the old view of channels, breaks of a trend line were universally considered to represent directional changes because there really wasn't any other way to interpret them. I have found this to be the case only a portion of the time, which probably accounts for much of the disillusionment in the old school of channeling. In reality, many breaks of channel boundaries end up as a change in slope rather than a reversal in direction—and that little acknowledgment alone may be enough to change the entire view of the use of channels. When channels change slope, they frequently overstep the prior boundary by a small distance but then reverse back rather than continue in the direction of the break. Thus, trading on the basis of channel breaks representing true reversals could have you frequently making your bet on the wrong direction entirely.

In Figure 11.4, the tentative channel break on the XLE is shown as dotted lines. Near the end of trading on February 10, the XLE came down, touched the lower line (perfectly) of the current short-term up channel (point F) at around 47, and bounced off that line to close near 48. On February 11, the XLE then traded down through the lower line all the way to 46, indicating a break. Before the day was over, however, XLE traded back up to the former line it just broke (point G), again hitting it with precision, and backing down. This *retest* pattern is very common in channel breaks and helps distinguish reversal breaks from slope changes. If the retest fails to come back up into the channel, then a reversal break is indicated. After trading lower on February 12, XLE moved back up and retested the former boundary line two more times on February 13, failing both times to penetrate. From this data, we are already able to draw a tentative new down channel to suggest the upcoming action in the XLE.

The trend break illustrated in Figure 11.4 was characterized by a sharp move downward from the upper line of the prior trend through the lower line and beyond. This is a common trend break scenario that leads to a new channel in the opposite direction of the prior one. Sometimes breaks occur with much less obvious vigor such as in **FIGURE 11.5**. Breaks of this nature will more likely turn out to be either slope changes or a channel widening than a reversal break. The fact that the latest peak did not reach the upper line of the existing channel and that there was no clear break and retest pattern are major clues that this is a change to the existing trend rather than a reversal break.

When price data moves outside a trend channel, it does not necessarily result in a break (i.e., a new reversal trend in the opposite direction). Several other scenarios are possible. The trend can be widening or changing slope. If changing slope, it remains in the same direction as before but bends to a lesser angle or even

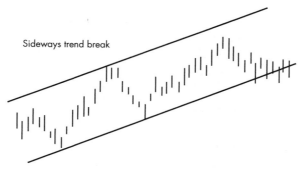

Sideways trend break

Figure 11.5   Sideways Trend Breaks

something horizontal. Slope changes are very common and are discussed in more detail below.

### OVERLAP

There is a persistent continuity between channels with most of them overlapping the previous ones. As you can see in Figure 11.4, the last leg of the existing short-term channel (from point C to point J) became the first leg of the new down channel for XLE. In slope changes, a channel may overlap by more than one leg with its prior slope.

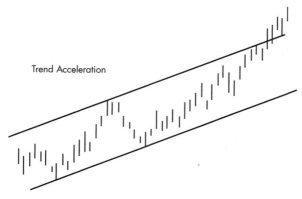

Trend Acceleration

Figure 11.6   Trend Acceleration

### CHANNEL LEGS AND INTERIORS

As noted earlier, the movements inside a channel are called *legs*. Most but not all legs will form their own channels, which I refer to as *mini-channels*. **FIGURE 11.7** illustrates the mini-channels of a short-term channel on the Nasdaq Composite Index.

Mini-channels are random in nature, taking on different shapes, widths, and slopes, but they do alternate between up minis and down minis. In this example, the minis all traverse the main channel completely from the lower to upper boundaries. Although this is common, it is not an absolute. A mini can stop short of the outer boundary and reverse in midchannel. Interior channel movements may not channel at all. They can "crawl" along a lower or upper line, or they can spike up and back down.

Mini-channels, however, are excellent short-term indicators and can offer clues on the health and nature of a trend as well as provide short-term trading opportunities. When a channel boundary is touched and the interior action reverses, the mini-channel changes in direction and takes on new characteristics (width, angle, etc.). These reversals form quickly and can confirm or deny that the overall trend is continuing or whether a break is imminent. Because they form in just a few hours, they can also provide

Figure 11.7   Nasdaq Composite (COMPQ) Twenty-Day Chart with Mini-Channels

Source: StockCharts.com

Figure 11.8   Powershares Crude Oil Double Long (DXO) Six-Month Chart

Source: StockCharts.com

excellent short-term trading opportunities. Also, a well-formed mini-channel can on occasion break or "push" the boundary of a larger channel (see **FIGURE 11.8**). After the break, the mini-channel generally remains intact, providing further clues and trading opportunities.

## SLOPE CHANGES

Recognizing that channels naturally bend or change slope is probably the single most important aspect of TCA. Without allowing for slope changes, it would appear that channels are frequently breaking out of their boundary lines but not reversing direction. Under the old view of trend channels, that would cause an observer to simply assume an old channel has broken and provide no way to explain the continued movement in the same direction. On the other hand, accepting that channels do frequently change slopes helps fill a huge gap of previously inexplicable time periods, and that in turn enables the observer to see that the market continually channels.

**FIGURE 11.9** illustrates how the SPX changed slope during the credit crash in the summer and fall of 2008.

The S&P 500 had been declining in a steady, long-term channel that began in 2007. Four lows—August 2007, January 2008, March

**Figure 11.9**  Standard & Poor's (S&P) 500 Fourteen-Month Chart

Source: StockCharts.com

2008, and July 2008—all fell on or extremely close to the lower line of that channel. That alone was a very telling chart, but in September 2008 the index lost its ability to even climb back to the upper line of that declining channel, indicating the possibility that the weakness was accelerating. Using the September high near 1300 as the second point of a new channel and connecting back to the May high, a revised slope could be drawn. Drawing a parallel lower line off the July low completes a revised channel that is slightly narrower and much steeper than the original. The newly formed channel (or an extension of the original, whichever way you prefer to view it) eventually came close to the September low and hit the October low right on the head.

This is an example of a change in slope that accelerates or steepens from the prior one. More commonly, however, a channel will yield to one with a lesser slope in the same direction, particularly if the original channel is somewhat steep to begin with. Trends tend to lose momentum over time much more frequently than they accelerate. It should not be necessarily assumed, though, that waning momentum is always followed by an eventual trend break and reversal. I have seen long running trends—in gold, for example—where a channel yields to another of lesser angle but then reaccelerates later.

It should also be noted that the May high points and the July low points anchored both sides of the channel together. That is not always the case. Only one line, or perhaps neither line, may necessarily anchor to the original channel at a convenient high or low point. In many cases, one or both lines of the new channel may cross the corresponding lines on the old channel in midair instead.

### REGRESSION LINES

Boundary lines are parallel to the linear regression line of a channel, but only after the channel is completely formed. Although parallel to the regression line, however, they are not necessarily equidistant from it. Until the channel is complete, the linear regression line cannot be expected to be parallel to the boundary lines as each additional leg of the trend (or portion thereof) alters the regression line. In the beginning of a trend, when only the first one or two legs exist, tentative channels can be drawn on high and low points, but at that stage the regression line is of no help at all in determining their slope.

### WIDENING AND NARROWING

In conjunction with slope changes, channels usually also widen or narrow. Steeper channels tend to be narrow, and flatter channels tend to be wider. Mini-channels can become very steep and narrow during a sharp move. Such moves are usually quick bursts that become part of a larger channel. Wider and flatter channels tend to be more sustainable over time.

### ANGLES

Angles (channel slopes) vary considerably, and there seems to be little relationship between the angles of oscillating channels, whether at the mini or short-term level. Mini-channels tend to have the steepest angles, frequently exhibiting 45- to 70-degree slopes. Short-term channels (the ones lasting days) tend to be much flatter (20 to 40 degrees) and long-term channels flatter still. Of course, there are exceptions, such as the sharp long-term downtrend of 2008–2009.

## REDEFINING THE CONCEPT OF SUPPORT AND RESISTANCE

TCA enables us to completely redefine the concept of support and resistance, one of the most basic and commonly used concepts in technical analysis. The current notion of support and resistance is that there are prices on both individual stocks and on the overall market indexes that tend to grab the general attention of market participants—typically a round number such as Dow 10,000 or a price at which either an individual stock or an index has turned previously. Such prices are gleaned from the charts themselves and represent little more than an artificial price at which either buyers or sellers have previously demonstrated they would step in. Often they are more apt to be figments of media hype than reality. A support level on a stock, for example, is merely an observed price at which buyers have previously been willing to purchase that stock. If a stock that has been trading between 50 and 55 for a number of weeks appears to attract buyers every time it slips down to 50, then 50 is deemed to represent support. The same effect can occur on a major index such as the 800 level on the S&P 500, which has formed some degree of support in the recent past. Such thinking is consistent with several of the behavioral tendencies described in Chapter 7.

Support or resistance price points will frequently be bolstered by good-til-cancel (GTC) orders that are placed ahead of time by many participants. In this instance, people might place a GTC buy order at a price of 50 under the premise that if it gets to 50 again they are willing to buy it there. If the stock trades down to 50, then the order executes; if not, then it just remains on the electronic order book at the exchange or with a market maker. Sellers may then build on the effect by placing stop orders to sell at a price just under 50. That rationale would hold that if the stock breaks 50, it would mean that buyers are no longer willing to support it there and that it would likely drop to a new support point a good bit lower. The sell-stop order executes as a protective strategy only if the stock trades down to the price specified on the order.

Defined in this manner, support and resistance levels on either stock or the overall market are largely a contrivance and wholly unreliable. They are caused by investors focused on them or being pointed to them by others. Since no one really knows how many buyers or sellers will be interested in a stock or in the market at a certain price, the concept is highly suspect. Most importantly, the only time an investor can point to support and resistance is after a turn has occurred in the same place more than once. Resist the urge to believe such claims, regardless of the source.

TCA explains support and resistance in an entirely different way, one that exposes support and resistance prices along a continuum relative to the current trend and a way that is determined by the unconscious behavior of thousands of people rather than the conjecture of a few outspoken ones. One has only to follow trend channels at the market level for a short while to be convinced that support and resistance are not determined by specific price points someone notices after the fact but are continuously represented by the outer boundaries of trend channels often before the fact. Furthermore, the support and resistance defined by trend channel boundaries can be incredibly precise.

**FIGURE 11.10** shows the same chart of the SPX as Figure 11.8 but without the channel lines and with the low points for the period identified.

There was not a single low that any investor could have considered support on this chart using the conventional definition because

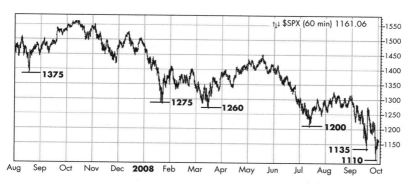

Figure 11.10    SPX Fourteen-Month Chart with Support Points

Source: StockCharts.com

each low was different. However, if you had been using TCA and drew the channels shown in Figure 11.7 after the first three data points, then you would have been able to project as many as five major lows and three major highs during this period!

## ADVANTAGES OF **TCA**

TCA provides an entirely new perspective on trend channels, turning them from an arcane, rarely used aspect of charting to a powerful technique for reading the market's behavior and forecasting not just direction but also potential lows, highs, and turning points. TCA provides both individuals and professionals with an objective glimpse into what the market is doing as reflected by all participants, and puts that picture into the context of time by showing us trends.

The fact that the market oscillates continually from up trend to down trend inside larger, longer-running trends that are always bounded by parallel lines is an astonishing discovery. The consistency and the frequent precision of TCA tell us that the phenomenon is real and persistent—in contrast to what the majority of financial scholars and investment professionals would have us believe. In conjunction with other technical indicators, the technique offers insights that should vastly improve investment performance for those who use it.

### *ADVANTAGES*

At a minimum, TCA's advantages as a market tool include the following:
1.  a continuous view of market trends over time;
2.  the ability to determine attractive entry and exit points for the market, regardless of whether you intend to trade or position for the long term;
3.  a context other than fundamental assessment in which to consider buy and sell decisions;
4.  a way to compare the relative attractiveness or risks of different markets;
5.  an early warning indicator for potentially substantial market risks or opportunities;

6. a way to focus on a single market index without needing a computer to roam the stock universe searching for ideas;

7. a methodology for investing and trading in any market environment; and

8. a technique that anyone can use and understand at little or no expense and with only a minor commitment of time.

## CHAPTER NOTE

1. Robert R. Prechter Jr., *Pioneering Studies in Socionomics* (Gainesville, GA: New Classics Library, 2003), p. 338.

# Putting It All Together **12**

*Buy and hold is dead. It's over. Game, set, match. Trend followers were the only ones who made money in the greatest market melt down since the Great Depression.*

MICHAEL COVEL

THOSE WHO DEVELOP trading techniques almost universally note the importance of establishing disciplined rules and parameters. Many quantify the parameters of both the strategy and the execution in extraordinary detail, leaning heavily on their computers for help. At one extreme, trend channel analysis (TCA) may be used in this manner, but the strength of its overall effectiveness lies in its ability to provide even casual investors with a perspective on the market that does not emanate from the media, a broker, or a know-it-all neighbor. The reason TCA is able to do this is that, at its core, it is a simple premise to understand.

The notion of human behavior and psychology as driving forces behind stock prices is sufficiently radical and complex to occupy scholars for many years to come. Indeed, we've only just learned that our behavior actually impacts prices much less the intricacies of how that happens. However, while the academics struggle to find equations that link herding instincts with market bubbles, TCA distills it down for us into usable fashion right now. That does not mean you simply draw a few lines and become wealthy. But it does mean you can see the big picture without a doctoral degree and without complex mathematics. I have been publishing free charts on Stockcharts.com for more than five years and have received unsolicited e-mail from hundreds of readers around the world who are unanimous in their view of TCA as a simple, intuitive, easy-to-understand methodology that provides surprisingly accurate results.

I admit that TCA is a relatively new concept (at least as it is currently being used), and we can expect it to undergo much more research and refinement. Rather than horde the technique until that happens, I have chosen to place it in the public domain so that it can spawn much more research than I could ever hope to accomplish by myself, thereby benefiting the most people. The technique should be flexible enough to be used in many different ways by many different people without fear of its effectiveness being diminished by widespread use.

## RESOLVING THE BULL AND BEAR CONUNDRUM

The notion of a bull market or bear market is a universal obsession, yet is entirely misconstrued, misinterpreted, and misunderstood by most people. For one thing, there is no universal definition for either term: they mean vastly different things to different people. For another, it is obviously a relative issue. In what time frame? In the context of what security or index? The market can easily be going up today, down in the near term, and up in the long term. Yet everyone gropes for a sense of whether the market is moving up or down (rest assured, it is always going one way or the other) as a context in which to make buy and sell decisions on individual securities, funds, or the like.

Noted market technician and money manager Richard Donchian began a long career in trend following in the 1930s, developing a proprietary channel technique using moving averages that still bears his name. Calculating moving averages by hand in the days before computers, Donchian was known for having said, "Nobody has ever been able to demonstrate to me that a complex mathematical equation can answer the question, 'Is the market moving in an up trend, down trend, or sideways?'"[1]

TCA handily resolves this issue by virtue of where current prices are relative to channels in different time views. One need only view

Figure 12.1    Dow Jones Industrial Averages (INDA) Two-Week Chart

Source: StockCharts.com

an index such as the Dow Jones Industrial Average (INDU) or Standard & Poor's 500 Index (SPX) in at least two different time frames to gain perspective on the current trend. While that perspective should never be construed as offering certainty, it can be viewed as valuable insight on current momentum and on where the boundaries lie that would indicate changes in that momentum if violated. Depending on the construct of the relevant channels, one may realize greater or lesser clarity at some times than at others and greater or lesser confidence in the likelihood of the next move.

In **FIGURE 12.1**, the upward trend channel of the DJIA is obvious in one-minute increments during a two-week period in late April and early May 2009. In this short-term channel, one would have been bullish for the short term, at least until May 11 when the channel broke.

But when the same index is viewed over a two-month period as in **FIGURE 12.2**, it can readily be seen that the entire channel bounded by lines 1 and 2 is a mini-channel within larger channel 5 and 6; that when the index reached point E in Figure 12.1, it touched the upper line (1) of the mini-channel as well as the upper line (5) of the larger channel, thereby increasing the chances of a reversal.

When the index broke the lower line (2) on May 11, the odds shifted in favor of a new down leg, even though it was still inside the

Figure 12.2   DJIA Two-Month Chart

Source: StockCharts.com

larger up trend. Accordingly, being bullish or bearish would have been a matter of your time horizon.

Author Nassim Nicholas Taleb has much to say on the subject of probability and market direction: "*bullish* or *bearish* are terms used by people who do not engage in practicing uncertainty." In addition, Taleb "could not understand the words *bullish* or *bearish* outside of their purely zoological consideration." His point is that absent a consideration for magnitude, direction can be misleading, as it is the probability of an occurrence multiplied by the potential magnitude of that occurrence that creates the statistical definition of expected return. While employed at a large investment house, he was once asked for a market opinion. He replied that he saw a 70-percent likelihood of the market rising during the following week. His colleagues then questioned why he had just boasted of holding a substantial short position in Standard & Poors (S&P) 500 Index futures. His reply was, "in the event of its going down, it could go down a lot."[3]

TCA offers perspective on magnitude by the width and steepness of channels, where width is considered the vertical distance between a channel's two boundary lines. The channel described by lines 1 and 2 in Figure 12.2 is about 250 Dow points wide. Therefore, as the index approaches an upper boundary line, one would have about 250 points of risk within the channel in the event the index traversed back to the lower line. (Vertically measured risk is the maximum risk in the channel. The flatter the path of decline between upper and lower boundaries, the less ultimate decline there is to a lower line touch.) As the index approaches point D and touches line 5 of the larger channel, the risk (or potential next move on the downside) becomes the width of the larger channel, which is closer to 600 Dow points. Naturally, at some point, every trend breaks; when that happens, the vertical risk from that point becomes the width of the ensuing down channel. In Figure 12.2, the break on May 11 ended up relieving the Dow Jones of roughly 350 points during the following week.

The bull and bear conundrum is pervasive. Media gurus proffer market projections at the drop of a hat, using naïve time frames like the end of the year or, worse, no time frame at all. Many of these projections are based on gross market valuations, previous highs, or just wild guesses. Such guesses tell us almost nothing and can be highly misleading, Most often, they are numbers without context, without likelihood, without margins of error, and often without time considerations. The channelist has a huge advantage not only in being able to project trends with accuracy and confidence in the first place, but also in evaluating the changing risk and reward profile within that trend (as boundaries are approached) and in being able to monitor price continually over time, knowing exactly when a trend has changed and being able to modify tactics accordingly.

## Using TCA

TCA is a tool, not a system. It can be used to support decision points for trading or positioning specific vehicles as well as to provide support for a variety of long-term investment strategies. Some examples are identified below.

### Long-Term Allocation

For long-term investors, TCA can be used as an allocation tool for broad asset allocation between equities, fixed income, and cash; for subclasses such as small cap or international stocks; and for industry sectors such as energy stocks or health care. For basic allocation

Figure 12.3   SPX Daily Chart 2005–2007

Source: StockCharts.com

decisions regarding the equity market, a long-term chart of a broad index such as the Standard & Poor's 500 will provide a picture of the long-term trend, enabling an investor to reduce equity exposure when the index is relatively high within its trend or increase it when relatively low. Using a chart such as the three-year chart of SPX in **FIGURE 12.3**, one might have increased equity exposure in the period of June through August 2006 when the lower channel line was touched, and then reduced equity exposure between June and July of 2007 when the upper line was touched. Two more opportunities would have occurred in 2007, increasing equity exposure again in August and reducing it in November.

For guidance on subclasses or sectors, the individual charts of those subclasses would need to be compared. If, for example, an investor wanted an allocation between large caps and small caps, the chart above could be compared to the chart of an index like the Russell 2000 (RUT). **FIGURE 12.4** shows the RUT chart for the same time period as the SPX chart above. A comparison of these would have shown that between October 2005 and May 2006, the RUT strongly outperformed the SPX on a relative basis. In fact, the RUT advanced about 25 percent compared with a 12 percent advance for the SPX. As the RUT was hitting its upper line, an underweighting in small caps would have been in order as the subsequent correction

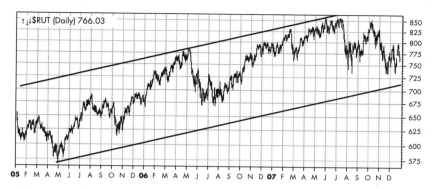

**Figure 12.4    RUT Three-Year Chart**

Source: StockCharts.com

in May and June shaved 7 percent off the SPX but 13 percent off the RUT.

Investors should remember, however, that hitting an upper or lower line does not guarantee that an index will traverse right back across the channel. However, an examination of the short-term channels inside this larger one would have provided additional guidance on the appropriate time to consider allocation changes.

### Risk Avoidance

While there is no equity-based strategy for avoiding risk altogether, having a mechanism for determining when the risks appear to out-weigh the rewards is extremely helpful, and TCA provides this by the very identification of a channel. The optimal time for evaluating downside risk is at the break of a channel, and an additional time is when a boundary line is touched in the direction of the trend (e.g., an upper line in a rising trend). Channel breaks result in either slope changes or trend reversals. Getting out or reducing exposure to long positions when an up trend breaks will keep an investor out of most down trends, though it will also keep them out of some up trends that have simply flattened in slope. For conservative investors, that may be a worthwhile trade-off. For the slightly less risk-averse, a strategy that waits to determine whether a break is the beginning of a new down trend and not just a slope change should still prevent falling into the biggest holes. **FIGURE 12.5** shows how much of the 2008–2009 decline might have been avoided if action was taken using the trend channels as guidance.

The SPX had been in a long-term up trend for several years, continuing into 2008, even with a more than 10-percent correction in July and August of 2007. The first break of that trend occurred in January 2008 at around 1400 on the SPX. Waiting to confirm whether the break would become a slope change (still heading upward) or new down trend only required waiting an additional two weeks or so as the SPX slid below 1375. An investor concerned about potentially greater downside would have exited at one of those two points. In late September 2008, an investor still could have exited when the trend accelerated downward (a serious danger signal) at around 1140. None of these exit points would have been easy to do emotionally after riding upward for several years, but the discipline of the channels would have kept the loss to a much lower level than was eventually seen.

Channels can occasionally accelerate in the same direction as the trend. Because of the market's alternating nature, however, breaking a channel in the reverse direction should be considered a possibility each time the index approaches the appropriate boundary line. This

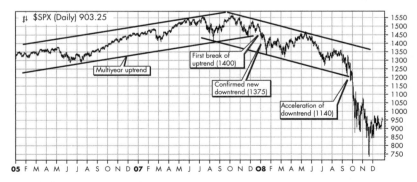

Figure 12.5   SPX Three-Year Chart

Source: StockCharts.com

makes action at the lower line of a rising channel more important as well as more difficult emotionally. To have exited the SPX at 1375–1400 after it traded over 1550 a few months prior was to realize an exit more than 10 percent below the peak. The SPX hadn't been that low since August 2007 and had rallied to new highs from there. Nevertheless, a huge potential loss could have been avoided by that exit. Investors who prefer the emotional ease of exiting at a high point can consider exiting long-term channels when upper lines are touched rather than waiting for lower lines to break. Some upside may be given up if the upper line touch is not the ultimate peak, but an investor who got out above 1500 in this situation would have been mighty glad.

### TAXABLE AND NONTAXABLE ACCOUNTS

The idea of liquidating stocks or funds described earlier to reallocate a portfolio or avoid risk unfortunately comes with the consequence of paying a possible capital gains tax if implemented in a taxable account. Qualified retirement accounts such as 401(k) plans or individual retirement accounts (IRAs) offer the advantage of avoiding those tax consequences. If you are buying into the market through a 401(k) plan into which you contribute from every paycheck, then you are dollar-cost averaging, a valid long-term approach to buying into the market. But you don't want to lose sight of the bigger picture. The contributions from each paycheck should not distract you from the value of your overall holdings. Buying into a falling market with a few hundred dollars per month is acceptable, but watching tens of thousands in value evaporate from the main holdings in the account is not. Even in a well-defined long running-up trend like the one in Figure 12.2, the width of the channel is about 200 points on the SPX or about 15 percent of the value in 2007. Think of that when you are at or near the top of the channel—that you have a 15-percent risk, even within the existing up trend. Should that up trend break and turn down (as it subsequently did in 2008), your risk would be considerably greater. Consequently, buying into equities with your regular payroll deferrals is fine, even in declining markets; but for your existing portfolio, following the rule above of lightening up (e.g., moving to bonds or cash) when upper channel boundaries are touched, or certainly when trends break, is a valid approach.

For taxable accounts, there are several ways to address the tax issue. Investors can position themselves in a long index fund or exchange-traded fund (ETF) on a major index like the S&P 500 and then use TCA to determine when to hedge the position rather than sell it. Hedging can be accomplished through the purchase of put options on that index, the sale of covered call options, or the offsetting purchase of an inverse index to counteract a decline in the one held. Of course, each of these hedging strategies requires that options or inverse ETFs are available on the desired instrument. Option approval is also required from your broker, but you would be engaging in the least risky option strategies and would generally be permitted to do so, even in an IRA account. If you are in mutual funds, then a hedging strategy would be more difficult to implement but could be done by using proxies such as puts on a broad index or sector that correlates highly with your portfolio. For example, puts on the Energy ETF (XLE) Spider would represent a good hedge to a portfolio laden with oil stocks. Each of these strategies involves other trade-offs. Put options can be expensive insurance, especially in a high-volatility environment. In addition, the appropriate duration and strike price and size of position need to be considered. In essence, this is the preferred hedging strategy for large institutional portfolios. Hedging with the purchase of an inverse ETF will require an amount of capital equal to the original long position, unless a double-inverse ETF is used, in which case half that amount would be required. With either the puts or the inverse ETF, a decline would result in a gain for the hedge, which would be subject to capital gains tax itself, and likely at the short-term rate.

I much prefer writing call options or a combination strategy involving call writing and put buying. But to write covered calls, you would need to own the underlying instrument, so a proxy would not work. Calls won't generally give you as much downside protection as the puts, but they will take in money rather than require an outlay, and they will enhance returns even if the market remains close to where it was or goes slightly higher. You can sell in-the-money calls for even greater protection if the situation warrants it. They also place time on your side, as opposed to the puts, which make you pay for time.

### EARLY WARNING SYSTEM

Imagine a windmill engineer studying the wind flows on a certain hillside and determining, from years of data, the optimal direction to face the windmill and the expected amount of electricity to be derived from the apparatus. Then envision him erecting the structure and enjoying several years of predictable, naturally supplied energy . . . until one day a hurricane comes along and blows the structure all over the hillside.

We tend as investors to get complacent, especially after years of "normal" market activity and positive returns. In doing so, we tend to lose sight of extreme or catastrophic risk. The 2008–2009 market may cure that tendency for a while, but it will return; it still exists now, even with the market down 40 percent in the last year. TCA can be used as an early warning system to help protect against such extremes. Little could have been done to foresee the unlikely events of September 11, 2001, but catastrophes such as the current financial crisis do take time to develop. TCA provides you with advance indications of increased risk or loss of momentum by continually showing you the market's behavior relative to prior time periods. If momentum is waning, then you can see it developing through slope changes or legs of channels that turn prior to reaching the outer boundaries. Even if you don't use the technique to trade or to change your allocation, you may want to keep an eye out for indications of greatly heightened vulnerability or opportunity.

As seen from Figure 12.4, a down channel existed on the SPX for nearly a year before accelerating into the abyss of the fourth quarter of 2008. Even if you had remained in the market until that time, you would have had the opportunity to react when the trend accelerated downward in September of that year. The market reaction to 9/11 came during an existing down trend as well. The crash of 1987 was a bit more of a surprise, although the channel did break on Friday before the market crashed on Monday. All things considered, there may be market shocks that offer no advance warning whatsoever, but for most market declines, there are warning signs for those who are willing to heed them, and TCA is one of the best (and most objective) tools available for generating such signals.

### TRADING

Short-term or swing trading strategies are ideally supported by TCA, particularly on major indexes and ETFs. The mini-channels offer explicit entry and exit points within the regular short-term channels and give very quick indications of breaks and turns. I have, on occasion, set price limits on buy or sell orders based on mini-channel lines and placed them early in the day when I knew I would be unable to monitor the market, and I have come back hours later and found profitable executions. Short-term channels also provide very quick evidence of a trend break, helping manage trading risk when going the wrong way.

Using options allows you to play both directions handily. The inverse ETFs and leverage ETFs are also very attractive trading instruments, though one needs to be very careful about the leveraged ETFs. Judging where a leveraged ETF will be when the normal ETF is at a certain price can be deceiving, especially when they work in percentages rather than absolute changes. In a high-volatility market, I have also found that I can buy ETFs and sell covered call options just days or weeks before expiration and reap an attractive return. Because of the alternation in mini-channels, there are continuous trading opportunities, even on the same security; but you can also shift between several index securities or sectors, affording ample opportunities almost every day.

Advantages aside, using TCA is still something of an art. If you are off by a line width, you can misread a signal. I therefore find it highly useful to watch a basket of indexes in order to see that there is consensus on channel structure and line placement. Indexes reach their lines at different times and where the SPX might land on a line, the Dow Jones might fall short or slightly penetrate. In addition, the higher beta (movement relative to the broad market) in small caps can make them a leading indicator as far as channels are concerned.

Lastly, one must always keep in mind that you are trading off tentative lines while a channel is developing; you must be careful not to get so focused on a line that you miss seeing a change or an alternate. I find it necessary to continually ask myself, "Is this the only realistic scenario or am I missing something?" I draw in possible alternatives whenever I spot them. Eventually, you will become more insightful and will spot clues on impending changes or see a channel pattern that just doesn't look right.

### LOOKING FORWARD

Advances in behavioral finance will no doubt continue as we have only scratched the surface on this bold new field of knowledge. At the same time, I expect to continue working on refinements to TCA because there will undoubtedly be many additional clues to market behavior hidden between the lines. Meanwhile, I fully expect others to uncover things I haven't seen as more and more people adopt a focus on both the behavior model and TCA.

### CHAPTER NOTES

1. Michael Covel, *Trend Following* (Upper Saddle River, NJ: Financial Times Press, 2007), p. 79.
2. Nassim Nicholas Taleb, *Fooled by Randomness* (New York: Random House, 2005), p. 101.

# Index

introduction of, 5
options on, 5
trend channel analysis of, 5–6

fair value. *See* intrinsic value
Fama, Eugene, 65, 70–71, 78
Fannie Mae, 166
fear of being left out, 141
Federal Reserve System, 141
Fibonacci series, 102
financial analysis, flaws of. *See* fundamental
    analysis, flaws of
financial marketing, 2
*Fooled by Randomness* (Taleb), 52, 73
framing, 127–128
Freddie Mac, 166
French, Ken, 159
Friedman, Milton, 112–113
fundamental analysis, flaws of, 17–18, 49, 89
    *See also* valuation
    buy recommendations, 26–29
    earnings estimates, 35, 65–66
    factors absent from, 41–44
    market timing and, 92–93, 96–97
    new market paradigm, 165–181
    overview of, 23–24
    today versus 1920s and 1930s, 30–31
    traditionalism, 25–37
    Wall Street's fixation on fundamentals,
        37–41
fundamental (theoretical) value, of an
    option, 170–171

gambler's fallacy, 128–129
Gann market cycles, 102
Garcia, Diego, 136
General Motors, 51, 145–146
George's heuristic, 140–141
Goetzmann, William N., 100–101, 104
going concern premium, 51–52
good-til-cancel (GTC) orders, 208
Google, 176
Graham, Benjamin, 23, 25
    *Security Analysis*, 30–31
Graham Joint Account, 31
Graham-Newman Corp., 31
Great Depression of the 1930s, 11–12

halo effect, 129–130
Hamilton, William Peter, 98–102, 104, 107

Hanks, Tom, 133
Harvard University, 117–118, 134, 150
Haugen, Robert A., 165
head games, trading and, 43
hedge funds, herding and, 132
hedging, trend channel analysis and, 222
Helmsley, Leona, 135
herding, 130–133, 141
heuristics
    affect heuristic, 123–124
    ambiguity aversion, 120–121
    anchoring, 121–123
    availability bias, 124–125
    belief perseverance, 125
    confirmation bias, 125
    conservative bias, 125–126
    disposition effect, 126
    endowment effect, 126–127
    framing, 127–128
    gambler's fallacy, 128–129
    halo effect, 129–130
    herding, 130–133, 141
    loss aversion, 133–134
    mental accounting, 134–136
    mood, 136–137
    overconfidence, 138–139
    other themes, 140–141
    overview of, 118–120
    quasi-magical thinking, 139
    representativeness, 139–140
    smart money effect, 131
    status quo bias, 127
    sunshine effect, 137
Hirsch, Jeffrey, 159
Hirsch, Yale, 145, 152–153, 159
Hirshleifer, David, 137
E. F. Hutton, 3, 25, 26, 28, 48–49

implied volatility, 171
index funds, 74, 76, 89, 101, 179–180,
    222
    changes in indexes and, 152
*Inefficient Markets* (Shleifer), 117–118
initial public offerings (IPOs), 28,
    42, 91
    as anomaly, 158
insider trading, 79
    reported, as anomaly, 157–158
Intel Corporation, 108–109
interiors, in trend channel analysis, 204

# About Bloomberg

BLOOMBERG L.P., founded in 1981, is a global information services, news, and media company. Headquartered in New York, Bloomberg has sales and news operations worldwide.

Serving customers on six continents, Bloomberg, through its wholly-owned subsidiary Bloomberg Finance L.P., holds a unique position within the financial services industry by providing an unparalleled range of features in a single package known as the Bloomberg Professional® service. By addressing the demand for investment performance and efficiency through an exceptional combination of information, analytic, electronic trading, and straight-through-processing tools, Bloomberg has built a worldwide customer base of corporations, issuers, financial intermediaries, and institutional investors.

Bloomberg News, founded in 1990, provides stories and columns on business, general news, politics, and sports to leading newspapers and magazines throughout the world. Bloomberg Television, a 24-hour business and financial news network, is produced and distributed globally in seven languages. Bloomberg Radio is an international radio network anchored by flagship station Bloomberg 1130 (WBBR-AM) in New York.

In addition to the Bloomberg Press line of books, Bloomberg publishes *Bloomberg Markets* magazine.

To learn more about Bloomberg, call a sales representative at:

London:    +44-20-7330-7500
New York:  +1-212-318-2000
Tokyo:     +81-3-3201-8900

# About the Author

RICHARD LEHMAN is an Instructor of both Finance and Derivatives at UC Berkeley Extension and a Vice President in the Wealth Management group at Mechanics Bank in Richmond, California. His financial career spans more than thirty years in Product Management, Marketing, Sales Management and Investment Management beginning with an eleven-year stint on Wall Street with E. F. Hutton, Thomson McKinnon and the New York Stock Exchange. Lehman holds a BS in Management Engineering from Rensselaer Polytechnic Institute in Troy, New York, and an MBA from the State University of New York at Albany.